More George!

More George!

Growing Up: The Story Continues . . .

Written and illustrated by

George Cunningham

 The **Hallamshire** Press 1994

*in association with George Cunningham
and Paul Hibbert-Greaves*

To Freda Hibbert, who made all this possible

© George Cunningham 1994

Published by The Hallamshire Press in association with
George Cunningham and Paul Hibbert-Greaves

The Hallamshire Press is an imprint of
Interleaf Productions Limited
Exchange Works
Sidney Street
Sheffield S1 3QF
UK

Typeset and produced by Interleaf Productions Limited
Printed in Singapore by Saik Wah Press Pte. Ltd

British Library Cataloguing in Publication Data

Cunningham, George
   More George
   I. Title
   759.2

   ISBN 1-874718-02-4

Contents

The Age of Progress	11
Voting Day	15
Oxford Conversation	20
A Warrior and Winter Warmers	24
What Pain it is to Part	28
The Crown and the Crooked Cross	33
Rejected	36
Britches, Books and an Interview	39
Mashings and Buffers	43
The Young Cellini	47
Grounded	50
Happy Birthday	52
The Phoney War	61
Bombs and a Bird	64
Two New Jobs	72
Training for Fire Fighting	76
Fire Watching, a Fylfot and First Aid	78
The Fighting 69th	83
In Town Tonight	89
A Fine Romance	94
A Night Out	99
Matters Military	106
The Big Race Day	110
The Beer Poacher	114
The Eternal Triangle	119
Posted	124
The End of a Romance	129
Victory in Europe (and Clarence Lane)	132

List of Colour Illustrations

Smith's Shop	watercolour	11
Marching Boys	pen and Ink	15
Pod's Downfall	pen and ink	18
Tommy Green's Drammer	watercolour	22
Whit March	pen and ink	29
Weston Park	pen and ink	30
Farewell	pen and ink	32
Three Wounded Soldiers	pen and ink	33
First Steps	watercolour	36
Buffer Lasses	watercolour	46
Joining Up	watercolour	51
Diggin' In	watercolour	52
In Hot Pursuit	pen and ink	55
The War Cabinet	watercolour	62
Bulldog's Warning	watercolour	64
The Moor in Flames	watercolour	68
The Moor Blitzed	watercolour	70
Fire Fighters	pen and ink	76
The Out-Patient	pen and ink	81
Britannia Outraged	pen and ink	86
Penny-a-Peek	pen and ink	90
Nell's Bar	watercolour	91
Rendezvous	watercolour	95
Blue and White	watercolour	99
Aubrey, the 'Owd Puff'	pen and ink	102
The Proposition	watercolour	109
End of the Line	watercolour	115
Defeated	watercolour	116
Helmut, P.o.W.	watercolour	117
Mrs Gumson's Wrath	pen and ink	122
Rocket Guns	watercolour	127
The Traveller's Rest	watercolour	130
Gone Forever	pen and ink	131
The Shaking of Mrs Podson	watercolour	134
Norman and Me	watercolour	137

Foreword

I AM VERY happy to report that, since I wrote the Foreword for the first edition of *By George!* seven years ago, George Cunningham is enjoying an even greater reputation as an artist of unmatched dedication, vigour and appeal. His paintings are sought by the most discerning of collectors and his limited editions by people from all walks of life. That first book was an instant success, and, due to demand, has now been reprinted. *More George!* is the long-awaited sequel, again featuring a collection of work especially created to accompany his reminiscences.

George's memoirs now take us through his adolescence in a war-torn Sheffield, where the character and humour of the Sheffield people still sparkled through the blackouts and the air raid sirens. We are treated to an engaging journey through his latter school years, his first job, and his humble part in the war effort. *More George!* is a funny, heart-warming story of a young man's life during a period that not only changed the world map but also a way of life for the inhabitants of a big industrial city.

While admiring his skills as an artist, we should not ignore George's talent for prose. In a deceptively effortless style, he has recreated in words the scenes that he first brought to life with his paintings — the delightful self-contained world of 1930s Sheffield, inhabited by a collection of colourful and wickedly detailed cameos of the characters he grew up with.

I think that the popularity of George's work lies in its universal appeal. It is so much more than mere nostalgia, although the careful detail of his paintings and his prose (and the dialogue!) will bring forth a surge of memories for those who were there. I believe that people of all ages and backgrounds are attracted by his wry observations that display a warmth and affection for humanity in all its peculiar manifestations.

I could not be more delighted with George's continued and deserved success. Dedicated though he is to painting, writing and burning the candle at both ends, he always has time for a friendly chat and a word or two of advice for an aspiring artist. It has long been a pleasure to know him as a friend, and I feel very proud to have been there to encourage him when he was still unknown.

I have no hesitation in whole-heartedly recommending that you delve into this second collection of George Cunningham's reminiscences. May I also express a hope that it is not the last.

Freda Hibbert

Freda Hibbert
Hibbert Brothers Limited

Preface

*T*HE YEARS from 1933 until 1945 were probably the most dramatic in modern history. They saw the rise of Adolf Hitler from a painter and obscure politician to the most powerful and feared dictator the world had ever seen, until his ignominious end in an underground bunker.

By a strange quirk of fate he was born in 1889, the same year as Charlie Chaplin, the world's best-loved comedian. Ironically, two little men, each with a small moustache and a funny walk, could on the one hand cause the massacre of millions, whilst the other made countless people laugh.

As always, Destiny deals some rum cards, and in this book I have written about my experiences during the period up to and including the war. No heroic exploits, no medals — except one for handwriting — but there again, few hardships and only occasionally a little danger.

In spite of worldwide battles and the blitz, Sheffield emerged from the conflict little changed. True, The Moor was devastated, but most of the houses, corner shops, cobbled streets, pubs and picture palaces still remained intact. The huge steel firms and cutlery factories employed thousands; trams trundled, people walked, and in the days before television, even engaged in conversation around the fireside.

Then came the architects and planners, who demolished thousands of homes, and in their wisdom insisted that the proper way for people (not them) to live was in high-rise flats. Almost overnight, it seemed, the Sheffield I had known for so many years disappeared. Dual carriageways replaced the cobbled streets, and tower-blocks surrounded by wasteland dominated what used to be tightly-knit, neighbourly districts, in which generations of the same families had been born, grown up, married, had children, and died.

Now the wheel has turned almost full circle. Many of the flats have been knocked down, and to replace them the planners' latest pipe dream — terraced houses — have been built. And to cap it all the tram is back.

George Cunningham

Chapter 1
The Age of Progress

AT THE corner of Clarence Street and Michael Road, Mrs Smith's shop provided our neighbourhood with most of the necessities of life. Butter, bread and cakes, jars of spice stood side by side with tins of John West salmon and Del Monte peaches, the highlight of the week for Sunday tea, and blue paper bags, plump with sugar, were kept well away from the bars of hard red carbolic soap and packets of mothballs.

One morning before school, my mother sent me across the street for a quarter pound of bacon for my father's breakfast and a small tin of Bile Beans for his liver. 'He says he feels a bit queasy this morning and they might buck him up,' she said, giving me a tanner, adding, 'Watch out you don't drop it down the grate.'

Behind the counter of the dark little shop, Mr Smith turned and smiled at me as the doorbell tinkled. He was a heavily-set, stocky man with a bushy walrus moustache and neatly-cut hair, parted and brushed across his forehead in the military style. In the shop he always wore the waistcoat and trousers from his navy blue serge suit under a brown smock, which he left unbuttoned. A gold Albert looped across his stomach into his bottom waistcoat pocket, from which he often produced with a stylish flourish, then a flick of the lid, a shiny gold hunter watch. According to Mr Smith, who never ceased to extol its virtues, there never was and never had been another timepiece with such accuracy. On one occasion, it was said, he was listening to a friend's wireless with his watch at the ready, and when the chimes

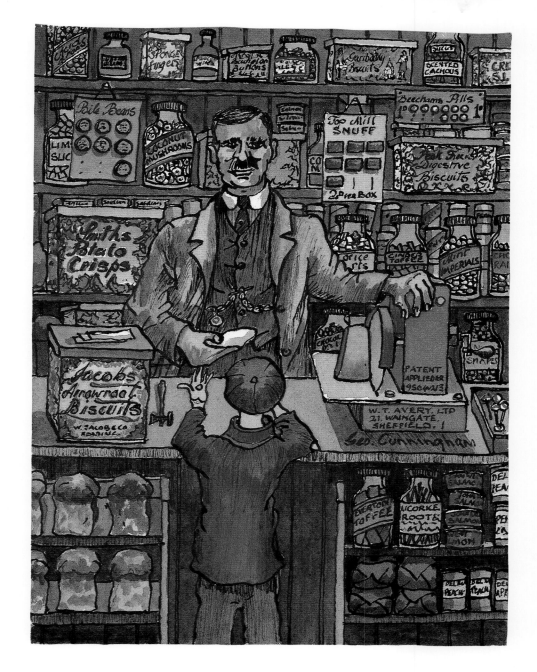

boomed out from London he nodded his head disparagingly and remarked, 'Big Ben's a bit slow tonight!'

His face lit up with a proud smile when I asked for the bacon, and, with the air of someone about to reveal a great treasure, he lifted a white linen tea cloth. 'What about that then? You're our first customer for the new bacon slicer.' I wasn't too pleased about this as I had been looking forward to Mr Smith's usual performance, honing on a butcher's steel a long thin-bladed carving knife which he tested for sharpness by shaving the hairs off his forearm. He put on quite a show for me, clamping the piece of bacon down on the spikes, then pushing the table forward as he turned the round steel blade. There was a quick swishy sound, and two or three rashers of bacon were neatly caught by Mr Smith in a sheet of greaseproof paper.

I told my mother all about this when I came back, but she didn't seem very impressed. 'I suppose he'll put the price up now to pay for the machine,' she sniffed, adding as she unwrapped the little parcel, 'It doesn't cut it as good as he used to with the knife. It's just like pink lint, there'll be nothing left when it's fried.'

My father swallowed the Bile Beans, gulping them down with a glass of water. He did look a bit yellow, even though the gas wasn't on. When his breakfast was put before him, he looked at the crisped-up bits of bacon and poked them around the plate with his fork. 'If this is progress, I don't reckon much to it,' he said, belching politely behind his hand as the pills took effect. 'What with flying round the world and one thing and another. It says in the paper we'll be sending rockets up to the moon in a few years' time. It's all baloney — even if they did land on it, they'd be stuck there forever.' When I asked him why, he chuckled and retorted, 'Because the moon's made of green cheese, didn't you know?'

Smith's doorstep was our relievo starting spot and it also came in handy for sharpening the wasters we got from the back of Richard's penknife factory in Broomhall Street. Its main function, though, was a meeting place for our gallant band — Vinny, Norman and me as founder members — and also because the top step could only accommodate three in comfort. Lit by a gas lamp in winter and warmed by the sun in summer, on its worn stone decisions were taken, serious matters discussed, expeditions planned and often carried out.

So it came about one Saturday morning we were sitting there. Norman was very impressed when I told him about the bacon slicer and how my Dad had poo-pooed the idea of rockets to the moon, but Vinny, who because he took the *Meccano Magazine* and had been given a *Boys' Own Annual* for his birthday considered himself better informed than us about such mechanical marvels, sucked air through the gap in his front teeth. 'Just wait,' he said, 'It'll not be so long before everybody'll have a car or even a plane. There'll be no more horses and carts blocking up streets.' To me this sounded rather disturbing, as I still derived some income from Moxay's manure business.

At that very moment, as if to belie Vinny's words, a distant rumble of wheels on the cobbles grew louder. It was obvious that something much heavier even than a railway dray was coming towards us, and I stood on the top step for a better view, whilst Norman tried to shin up the gas lamp. Vinny made out that he wasn't interested by looking up in the sky, but even he was startled when around the corner from Moore Street came a pair of oxen pulling a large covered wagon. Ponderously, the huge horned beasts, their doleful-eyed heads swaying in a slow rhythm from side to side, ambled towards us down Clarence Street. The driver, perched aloft with both feet on the buckboard, held up his whip in what could have been a salute, or what was more likely a warning to us not to jump up behind. The wagon's canvas sides, as high as the bedroom windows they were passing, had the words 'Atora Beef Suet' emblazoned in large letters.

I thought that I would air my knowledge a little and stated, 'I bet it's one o' them Boer wagons. He'll be trekkin' to Cape Town.' 'Naow 'e int,' retorted Norman, ''e's guing dahn t' Stores at bottom o' road —

arve seen 'im theer befoor.' Vinny was even more put out when a few minutes later a smart, highly-polished, dark green Rington's Tea cab, pulled by a spirited chestnut bay, rolled past us at a spanking pace. 'By Gum, 'e can shift!' exclaimed Norman, excitedly. 'I don't know so much,' Vinny sniffed disparagingly, 'Malcolm Campbell in the Bluebird can do three hundred miles in an hour, while that horse is doin' ten.'

'Aar, but 'e aint gorreny tea t' deliver, 'as 'e?' countered Norman. Not to be outdone, Vinny pointed up to the sky as a biplane flew over us, trailing a long streamer advertising Alan Cobham's Flying Circus. 'That's what I'm going to do!' he declared. 'It's a lot safer than a rotten old horse and cart!'

Chapter 2
Voting Day

OVER THE last few days posters had been posted on walls and hoardings proclaiming the forthcoming Municipal Elections. On voting day, after tea, the three of us assembled in Norman's back yard. We all had the regulation equipment for such an important occasion: two empty tin cans apiece. I had rummaged in our dustbin and found a Nestle's condensed milk tin and a larger one that had once contained Cirio tomatoes. I rinsed them out under the tap, tucked in the jagged lids and tried them out for sound, nodding with appreciation at their volume and resonance.

Norman had a Burgon's sliced peach can and a Parsley brand salmon tin, and Vinny appeared from his house with a matched pair of Tate and Lyle's Golden Syrup tins, carefully washed and polished by his mother. The march we were about to embark on was the traditional route passed down by generations of voting day supporters. This was round the lump, which meant tramping down Clarence Street, along Hurst Road, up Humble Road and back on to Michael Road, with an occasional variation down to Bridgefield Road. The three of us had formed up in good order, line abreast, at the corner of our house. Vinny raised his hand to give the signal for us to strike up the band and start the march, when down the street at a shambling trot came Albert Moxay.

His attire was informal; although it was a warm evening he sported a thick woollen maroon-coloured jersey, with snot-stiffened sleeves and a large hole in the front. Over his shoulder was a loop of clothesline from which hung a billposter's bucket. 'We aint gorreny tins at ar 'ouse.

A fon dis in street at side orra barrer,' he told us, brandishing a large possing stick, which he thumped on the side of the bucket, making a dull unmelodious sound, which could only have been produced by such an unusual musical combination.

At first Vinny flatly refused to let him join us because he wasn't properly equipped but, when I suggested that Moxay could march behind and beat out time for us, he reluctantly agreed. 'On third stroke,' shouted Norman, who had promoted himself up to second in command.

'Thud! thud! thud!' went the drum and off we marched in a steadfast rank of three, heads held high, waiting for the signal which was not long in coming. With a resounding clang of his Tate and

Lyle's, Vinny led us into the time-hallowed election day refrain, every word accompanied by the melodious clang of our cans.

Vote, vote, vote for Mr Jowett,
CLANG, CLANG, CLANG, CLANG, CLANG, CLANG
You can't vote for a better man.
CLANG, CLANG, CLANG, CLANG, CLANG, CLANG
For Jowett is the man,
CLANG, CLANG, CLANG, CLANG, CLANG
We'll have him if we can,
CLANG, CLANG, CLANG, CLANG, CLANG, CLANG
And you can put old Simpson
CLANG, CLANG, CLANG, CLANG, CLANG, CLANG
In your old ash can!
CLANG, CLANG, CLANG, CLANG, CLANG

Twice around the lump we marched, curtains were parted, people came to their doors and two little lads who were playing at hopscotch stopped their game and cheered us on. We swung smartly into Michael Road in good order, ready for another round. At the back of Pickering's cardboard box factory two of their big Ford vans, with the canvas tops rolled back, were being loaded up with kids under the supervision of Mr Truelove, the managing director. Although we had no idea who the candidate's party was whose name we had been chanting, he must have had Mr Truelove's support because he beckoned to us and helped us aboard.

Walt Bradshaw, the driver, swung the starting handle, heaved himself into the cab very nimbly, in spite of his gammy leg, and off we went for an electioneering cruise around the streets. Our van led the way along Moore Street and, with the backing of about thirty untrained voices and our band, Mr Jowett's victory seemed certain.

Down Young Street, past the tarry smell of Lister's asphalt works, The Industry Inn, and on to Matthew's chip shop rolled our merry ensemble, blissfully unaware that we were entering enemy territory. The first sign of this was a warning shot across our bows, or, to be precise, a tin can filled with a liquid that, hopefully, was only water. It whizzed over Moxay's cropped head and exploded on the back of the cab, liberally sprinkling the choir, creating momentary panic then expressions of disgust as the contents of the can made itself known to the nasal organs. Instinctively I had ducked down below the van side, but not before I spotted the would-be assassin. Moxay did as well, because we both shouted at the same time: 'That wer Pod!' On hearing our approach along Moore Street he must have lain in ambush in the pub doorway, our noise giving him ample time to fill his noxious grenade.

Shaken but undeterred, we continued our journey in good style back to the cardboard box factory, where we disembarked to make room for another cargo of eager voyagers. We decided to make one more tour before calling it a day, so for a change of route down Humble Road, we went and started to turn the corner at Mrs Timbo's shop into Bridgefield Road, putting Mr Simpson into the old ash can with great gusto and feeling. Just as we finished and were gathering breath for another stanza, I heard a louder rendering, putting *our* candidate into a similar receptacle. With a backward glance I was startled to see a party of four or five lads, equipped with cans as we were and led by Pod.

Billy Podson, whose family had recently flitted from the Wybourne into Green Street, had just started at our school, but his reputation had preceded him. He was two years older than me, podgily but strongly built, with large hands and wrists so thick one wondered how he managed to get his jacket on and off. A sallow, spotty face topped with greasy, lank hair was complemented by small brown stumps of teeth and an outward cast in each eye, which came in useful when he was about to thump anyone, which he frequently did, because his victim thought that Pod was looking somewhere else.

Our voices tailed away into a few stumbling words as Pod's gang advanced towards us. This encouraged them to a louder clanging and, when they were twenty yards away, Pod let fly with his tin can. A barrage opened up from both sides. The air was full of flying metal. Norman received a direct hit on the head from a corned beef tin with the key still attached. Vinny copped a cocoa tin which exploded on impact, full in the chest, blowing off the lid and scattering brown dust all over his shirt front. I was more fortunate: a pea tin struck me a glancing blow on the shoulder, giving me a fright, but what I thought was blood dripping from my cheek was a green liquid. I flung my tomato can and missed, then followed up with the condensed milk, which Pod contemptuously parried with a beefy paw. Things were getting desperate: our ammunition was gone and we were outnumbered two to one.

Panic turned my legs to water and wild thoughts flashed through my brain. Should I surrender and throw myself to the mercy of the enemy, or run for it, only to be caught and tortured? Pod, at the head of his victorious army, grinned malevolently. Which of us would he thump first? I shuddered to think, as he swaggered slowly towards our cowering little band, savouring his hour of triumph. His eyes, which appeared to be looking at both sides of the street, were horrifying, even more so when he turned his head sideways and focused one of them on me.

'Narden, big 'eead,' was his opening pleasantry, which upset me even more. I knew that I had rather a large head, but not nearly so big as Tommy Tinley's, who once confided in me that his father used to clout him across it, complaining that it had spoilt his Saturday night's enjoyment. A last vestige of courage welled up inside me and I squeaked defiantly, 'Shurrup, cockeye!' This enraged Pod so much that he brandished his fist and charged full tilt at us. In a blind panic I turned to run, when, from behind, a sturdy arm shoved me to one side.

As I stumbled and nearly fell, I saw that it was Moxay, who I thought had deserted during the battle. He had unlooped the rope from his shoulder and with it he swung the billposter's bucket in a mighty arc and then let go. It cleared the cobbles by inches and took the running Pod full across his shins. There was a resounding clonk and an agonised screech of anguish as he cannoned back into his troops, taking two of them to the ground with him. 'Cum on!' shouted Moxay and off we ran up Humble Road, never stopping until we reached the safety of Norman's yard. 'Good owd Moxay,' I gasped, 'That showed 'em.'

Vinny went into his mother's house and came out wearing a clean shirt and carrying a plate full of halves of bread cakes spread with best butter and golden syrup. Sweet were the fruits of victory. I licked my sticky fingers, looking longingly at Vinny's half-finished slice, wishing he'd give me a bite.

Then Moxay made my blood run cold. 'Pod'll gerris own back, don't thee worry.' He was usually right in military matters and I wished he would stay with us, but off he went, banging his possing stick on house walls and the odd door, no doubt causing some trepidation to the occupants.

Chapter 3

Oxford Conversation

ONE OF father's favourite tipples was John Smith's Magnet ale, a rich, heady, ruby brew from Tadcaster. As a change from Stones' at Mr Broadley's or Gilmour's at Kenny McLeod's, he occasionally sent me up for some to the Oxford House at the corner of Moore Street and Clarence Lane. At least the pub sign said it was so called, but it was better known as 'Tommy Green's', the name of the landlord. One evening in late summer I came home, sweating a little after a few games of relievo. On the table was the quart jug, and my father was twiddling a shilling between his fingers. 'Just pop up to Tommy Green's and get me three gills of Magnet, there's a good lad. Here's a bob, you'll want three ha'pence change,' he said.

I went the long way round, up past Wilson's the grocer's at the corner of Clarence Street and Mr Jessop's milk shop on Moore Street. He was swilling out and waved to me from the bright, white shining clean interior of his little house window dairy. I wondered why my father didn't drink pints of milk instead of beer, which was so much dearer. When I grew up I vowed that I would, thinking longingly of cool, fresh, sweet milk in contrast to the harsh, bitter taste of beer, which I sometimes craftily tasted.

The tall narrow doors of Tommy Green's dram shop opened easily at the touch of the worn brass sneck. The room, if it could be called that, was about a yard wide and made even narrower by a well-scrubbed white wooden bench, which ran its length up to the bar. A high, dark oak partition separated this little off-sales from the drammer. A large mirror behind the bar gave me a good view of the customers

and I could quite clearly hear their conversation. A domino school was in full swing and standing at the bar Harry Hill the hawker was holding up against the light a newly-pulled pint of beer, quizzically eyeing its clarity.

Tommy Green called out to everyone in general, 'I'll not be a minute. I'm gunner put a new barrel on.' Harry looked relieved at this and put his untasted drink on the bar. I lolled against the partition, wondering what was for supper. Perhaps Dad would give me the odd ha'penny for some chips if I was lucky. The rattle of dominoes being shuffled for another game ceased, as the players, by mutual consent and also to prevent any cheating, went out of the room and down the passage to the gents. A familiar voice, quite audible, sounded close to my ear, as indeed it was, because when I craned my neck I could see reflected in the mirror, seated at the other side of the partition, Mrs Gumson and her bosom friend, Nellie Slatter.

There was, for once, after the last words I heard, an unusual break in the gossip between the two ladies. Mrs Gumson, easing her ample bulk into a more comfortable position, took a delicate swig from her glass, rearranged her coverall with a movement altogether feminine and remarked, as if casually, 'A see Alice Higgins an 'er 'usband Percy 'av packed it in then.' On hearing this dramatic news, Nellie, who had been chewing her fingernails in contemplative boredom and with her head to one side was working her teeth around a difficult bit on her thumb, stopped and became all ears.

Wide-eyed, she turned to face her companion, 'Oo, wot d'yer mean?' she gasped. 'Thive only bin wed six month, wot's wrong we 'em?' Mrs Gumson, not to be hurried now that she had the full attention of her listener, replied weightily, 'Not *them*,' then with great emphasis, ''Im, 'ee weren't up to 'job!' A stunned silence of the fair Nellie was broken when she breathed, 'Yer don't mean that theer?' 'Yers,' was the reply. 'Alice went to 'slisseter 'n 'ee telled 'er she could gerra divorce, becuss marridge was niver constipated!' Relishing in her

role and well pleased by the effect these words had caused, she continued, 'Percy's tekken up wi a big coil man from Pitsmoor an' gone ter live wi 'im.'

Nellie, righteous anger bringing her wide-open mouth back into action, exclaimed, 'The dirty little dog, 'ee ort t'be flaming well 'ung!' Mrs Gumson moved her head slowly and ruminatively from side to side. 'That wor trouble wi 'im. Alice towd me.' She mused, casting her eyes down to the empty glass that she had drained in her emotion, ''Ee int!'

Emitting a self-pitying sigh, she continued, 'Ar allus thowt thi wer summat queer abart that little sod. Arm sure it were 'im wot pinched mar best bloomers offa line a bit sin.' Nellie nodded her head in agreement and patted her friend's thigh consolingly. 'Neer mind luv, thieves never prosper, thi'll do 'im no good.' Mrs Gumson, though visibly affected by this expression of friendship, was cheered by the sight of Nellie fumbling for money in her purse and chuckled, 'Ar bet that bloody coil man has a reight job wi 'em — elastic in legs were erer s'tight!'

Engrossed by this illuminating conversation, puzzled by what 'that theer' meant and what particular job the diminutive Percy 'wasn't up to', I was even more intrigued by what he could do with the ample Mrs Gumson's voluminous undergarments, which I had often seem billowing on her clothesline.

The domino school returned and resumed play. Mr Green ascended from the nether regions, pulled off a few pints, then replaced the mollified Harry Hill's drink, explaining 'It wer bottom o'barrel,' and took my jug. All the way home down t'owd lane and past Beeley's Foundry, I was puzzling out what I had overheard and meant to ask my father and mother a few pointed questions when I got home.

Once there, I had just got started, asking what job Percy wasn't up to, when my father, looking quite startled and mother, blushing, put the change, all of it, back in my hand and giving me a hurried but

affectionate push to the door said, 'Go and get yourself a penny fish and a ha'porth of chips.'

I couldn't understand this unexpected bonanza and thought about saving the penny and just having a ha'porth of chips, but conscience prevailed and I lashed out all the lot. I walked round the lump eating them and savouring the last bit of batter to be washed down by the vinegar that had drained into the bottom of the paper. When I got home again, Dad had his head buried in the *Telegraph and Star* and mother gave my chest a brisk rubbing with camphorated oil, which made it difficult for me to ask any questions. Anyway, I was so sleepy and replete with food that I was glad to stumble upstairs and fall into bed, to dream of an irate Mrs Gumson armed with a clothes prop, chasing Percy down her entry.

Chapter 4
A Warrior and Winter Warmers

THE YEAR was 1934. I was ten years old and could look forward to the future with a certain amount of complacency, based on the fact that I had amassed two shillings and threepence ha'penny from Whitsuntide, the fertiliser business and running errands. On top of all this I won a leather football and a silver medal in a handwriting competition sponsored by my favourite books, the *Wizard*, *Hotspur*, *Adventure* and *Skipper*. The ball replaced our makeshift brown paper one and the standard of play increased considerably, as did my status when I displayed my medal.

Harry Flathers, an acknowledged expert in precious metals due to an apprenticeship with his father, grudgingly admitted after subjecting my medal to a rigorous test with his eyeteeth, 'It's or reight. Ar'll gie thi tuppence forrit.' Sorely tempted though I was by this vast sum, I declined, thinking that I could hold my award in reserve in the event of my capital running out, or the fertiliser business collapsing, leaving me skint.

Christmas seemed to come much quicker now and the school holidays didn't seem to last as long: both signs of my advancing age. Summer came and went and autumn in its turn, then winter with its dark nights and the return of my cough duly made its appearance. As a precaution against another attack of pneumonia, mother coated my chest with a thick layer of goose grease covered by a square of red flannel. This was removed on Friday bath night and after my ablutions a new layer was applied. It was quite warm and comforting, although by the end of the week it became a trifle malodorous.

The frost burst a water pipe outside Sweetmeat Joe's spice shop in Clarence Street and made necessary a large hole, smoky paraffin warning lamps, a night watchman complete with box and, best of all, a large coke brazier. Vinny, Norman and I soon established friendly relations with the guardian of the hole, who said his name was Ernest Watchorn. He told us this when I asked him, as I was always inquisitive about people's names. He gave a little chuckle when I remarked brightly 'It should have been Watchfire, because that's what you do!' A sparsely-built man with a long nose, sunken cheeks, a quiff of hair beneath his cap neb and a bushy moustache, he had some difficulty in sitting down and getting up. This was due to the fact that he had only one sound leg, the other ending above his knee, the stump covered by his pinned-up trouser leg. As our acquaintance blossomed into friendship, he confided to us that he had 'Copped a packet on Somme' and that he had been fitted out with an artificial leg, but couldn't get on with it. 'It wor too ockud, it used ter bend when ar dint want it to an' straighten art wheniver it fancied.' He sucked reflectively on a Woodbine tab-end, which he lit with a spill of paper from the fire, holding his head sideways in case he burnt his 'tache. Once upright he could move at a surprising speed with the assistance of a crutch — of which he seemed very fond, because every now and then he bestowed on it a friendly rub with a large red-spotted handkerchief, in which he also used to carry his dinner basin. 'It's saved me a bob or two, has this,' he said, giving the crutch an extra burnish with his coat sleeve. 'Ar Jack lost his other leg at Wipers, so we buy a pair o' boots between us, 'n 'e as one 'n I 'ave t'other.'

Inside his hut, wrapped in sacking, he kept a shovel, the blade of which was brightly polished and greased with dripping. Promptly at six, by the Co-op clock, Mr Watchorn raked the brazier into a steady glow and, with the aid of a steel spike stuck in the ground, placed the shovel on the fire. From a biscuit tin he produced four rashers of bacon, two thick slices of bread and an egg. He laid the bacon in the form of a square on the blade of the shovel, winking one eye mysteriously at our inquiring looks. A toasting fork, made from twisted wire, held the bread up to the heat, the bacon, spluttering nicely and sending out a mouthwatering aroma, was turned with the aid of an army knife, and into the four-sided square of bacon Mr Watchorn deftly cracked the egg. The toast was done only on one side and on the other the bacon and egg were neatly slid off the shovel and entrapped between the two slices. A mashing can full of water with tea, condensed milk and sugar in it was suspended over the fire to be ready when Mr Watchorn had finished his sandwich.

After his meal, he picked his teeth with a sharpened matchstick, belched contentedly, thumped his chest, lit a fag and said, 'Ar'll show yer summat, nar.' He fished in his inside jacket pocket and produced the thinnest wallet I had ever seen; it was like two pieces of brown paper stuck together. 'See that?' he exclaimed, holding it up for our dubious admiration. 'Ar Ernest, 'im that wor in City Battalion, 'ad it made in Mespot an' when thi wor drafted o'er t'France for Big Push wi' us, we met behind line in an estaminet.' His eyes misted over and he had to light another Woodbine before he continued. 'Funny it wor my twenty-first birthday, so 'e gen me this wallet.' I wasn't very impressed, and even less so when he carefully opened the wallet and just as carefully fished into a little compartment and produced, between thumb and forefinger, a tiny object.

He held it near the firelight, so that we could all see it more clearly. It was half of a tiny wishbone, about as long as my little finger and not as thick. He laid it in the palm of his hand for our inspection, enjoying our mystification. 'Even in Civvy Street, ar Ernest was allus a scrounger, an' when we cum art o' that Froggy boozer he undid his pack and pulled art a chicken e'd pinched from kitchen at back o' pub. We wor well behind line so we lit a little fire in a shell 'oil and boiled it in a dixie.'

He chuckled at the recollection and remarked, 'It wor tough as leather an' a bit o' gravy wud 'a 'elped, but it went darn awreight. Then we pulled wishbone fer luck an' ar won.' A little silence followed, then Mr Watchorn said, 'Ar kid asked me if ard made a wish 'n ar said ar wished it 'ad been a bigger chicken!' We all laughed at this, but he quelled our mirth somewhat by saying 'Wot ar did wish for wor that ar kid would cum back in one piece. 'E wor only nineteen, 'e'd gen is wrong age when 'e joined up.' Again he was silent and had to light another fag before he could continue. 'Two days later on, on first o' July, 'e went o'er top, 'n they brought back wot wor left on 'im in a bag.'

Lost in our own thoughts, we all gazed into the fire. I wondered what I could say to console Mr Watchorn, but he solved my problem by suddenly exclaiming, 'Ever made a winter warmer?' A shake of the head from me, a blank look from Norman and a non-committal suck of teeth from Vinny convinced our host that we didn't know what he meant. The materials were readily available. We each gouged a lump of clay from the hole and under Mr Watchorn's instructions fashioned an open-topped box about the size of half a brick. At one end a hole was made with a finger, then the creation was laid near the fire. Impatiently we waited as Mr Watchorn carefully pinched the clay, testing it for hardness. At last he nodded his head. 'They're abart reight,' he informed us and from the back of his hut produced some kindling wood broken off a gatepost in an advanced state of dry rot. This he carefully shredded into our boxes, making sure the hole was free. Then came the big moment. With a spill of paper he lit the kindling, handing the boxes to us, one at a time. 'Na then!' he ordered, 'Blow! Not too hard, else y'll blow bloody lot art, 'n fer Pete's sake, don't suck.' We puffed and puffed and soon a friendly glow and then a lovely warmth spread through the box.

What with this and the heat from the brazier, the goose grease had started to melt and run down my stomach giving cause for some

enquiring sniffs from Norman and Vinny. I was basking, baking and blinking in a delicious euphoria, my overcoat buttons almost too hot to touch, when through the shimmer of heat above the fire I saw on the Stores clock that I should have been home half an hour ago. Bidding a hurried farewell to my friends, I dashed up the street to Michael Road. Our doorknob had always been a bit wonky, so I shoved the winter warmer in my coat pocket to enable me to use both hands. I mumbled some excuse to my father and mother and hung up my coat behind the door on the cellar head. I started to tell them about my new-found friend, the night watchman, but they were listening to 'Stainless Stephen' on the wireless and shushed me into silence, so I sat quietly reading *The Skipper*. After a few minutes I was nodding off, when Dad started up from his chair, rushed across the room and flung open the cellar door. Smoke and the acrid smell of burning cloth made him cough and brought tears to his eyes as he held up my coat and pulled out the winter warmer and what was left of the pocket lining. I was sent to bed with no supper, admonished by my parents and a complaining chesty chirrup from Charlie the canary. Next day though, at school, I was the centre of attraction, showing off the burnt hole and casually remarking that last night we'd had a fire at our house.

Chapter 5

What Pain it is to Part

*T*HROUGH ALL the trials and tribulations of my early life, my friendship with Norman Blackwell, but more particularly with Vincent Crookes, remained ever constant. In hard-fought games of football and cricket, expeditions to remote parts of the globe like Bell Hagg, and many street battles, we had stood resolutely shoulder to shoulder.

One Whit Monday morning we were to be part of a parade from St Silas Church up to Weston Park for the Whitsuntide Sing. Clad in our still uncomfortably stiff new suits, we gathered in the church for a short service, conducted by the vicar, Mr Haythornthwaite. Pink-faced and benign, he led us in a rousing rendition of a hymn, which I enjoyed but couldn't understand some of the verses, such as:

> *I will not cease from mental fight*
> *Nor shall my sword sleep in my hand,*
> *Till we have built Jerusalem*
> *In England's green and pleasant land.*

On a wall in our school was a large coloured picture entitled 'Jerusalem from the Mount of Olives'. It showed three shepherds gazing down towards a temple and a huddle of little white houses. I could understand why they would want to build in England, because the countryside was parched and barren, with only little scrubby thorn trees and strewn with stones and boulders. It would be a right job trying to play football or cricket amongst that lot; it wasn't a patch on the field at Endcliffe. I bet there wouldn't be any trams, gas lamps, chip shops, spice shops and picture palaces either, in the new Jerusalem.

The service over, we formed up in the cobbled streets outside the church. Banners were hoisted, billowing gently in the breeze, and, led by the Boys Brigade Band, off we marched.

In Upper Hanover Street we were joined by reinforcements from St Andrew's Church, who were led by their minister, Mr Nicol. Hounsfield Road was a bit of a pull, but we were encouraged by a tram which led our procession. The driver gave us a parting farewell clang on his bell as he was turned off by the pointsman near the Scala Picture Palace. On past the University and through the gates of Weston Park we sallied, under the watchful gaze of Ebenezer Elliott and the War Memorial to the York and Lancs. Albert Moxay, who wasn't in church but had somehow managed to join the procession and fall in beside me, looked up at the statue of the soldier and cried out, 'Dat looks like mi fadder up theer, 'e 'ad a dint in 'is tin 'at when 'e cum hooam from waar!' Hundreds of children and grown-ups in their Sunday best were on the grass lawns surrounding the bandstand. Hymn sheets were handed out and we were led by a gentleman in a high winged collar playing a harmonium, the notes from which were wafted by the stiff breeze into a crescendo of sound, or sometimes a near silence.

This is more like England's green and pleasant land, I thought, eyeing the 'candles' on the conker tree in front of the Mappin Gallery, trying to count what the harvest would be in autumn. The meeting dispersed. Norman, Vinny and me trailed back down Hanover Street and crossed over Ecclesall Road to Hastley's herbalist shop, where we

lashed out some of our Whitsun money on a pint of sarsaparilla apiece. It was then, probably due to the stimulus of this heady brew, that Vinny dropped a bombshell by announcing 'We're flitting soon up to Thorpe House estate, mi dad's bought a house up there.' I had never dreamt that anyone could possibly have enough money to buy a house. Everybody, I thought, paid rent to a man like our landlord, Mr Harrop, who came round weekly in his trilby hat and long raincoat, with an umbrella hooked over his arm, book at the ready. In fact, it was said about some of the people in Young Street that if they had paid their rent two weeks running, the police came round to enquire where they had got the money from.

The day came soon enough for Vinny's departure. Speight's van, with three men in rolled-up shirt sleeves and green baize aprons, moved tea chests full of crockery, sideboard, table and dresser with deceptive ease, even though they had to take out the bedroom window to slide the wardrobe down a ladder. Some of the neighbours were gathered around at a discreet distance, making approving remarks or quizzical grimaces at the quality of the furnishings, whilst others, betrayed by the twitch of a curtain, kept up their observation from indoors.

Vinny and his brother George followed the van along Michael Road to make the journey

JAMES LAVER
& SONS LTD
BUILDERS AND CONTRACTORS
THORPE HOUSE ESTATE
SEMI DETACHED
VILLAS
AT £370 EACH
DEPOSIT £35
REPAYMENTS
FROM 9/9 WEEKLY
NO ROAD, LEGAL, OR
MORTGAGE COSTS

Geo. Cunningham

Bottom, thundered under the railway bridge, sailed past the Coliseum, then groaned up the steepness of Chesterfield Road to Derbyshire Lane. It was a long trek up to the estate and I wished that I had brought something to eat and drink, but finally we came in sight of a big wooden board, which advertised houses for sale by Lavers. Painted on it very artistically was a picture of a young couple walking into a sunrise and underneath them were the prices of the houses.

I had Vinny's address on a piece of paper, and although some of the roads were still unmade and builders' tackle lay everywhere, we reached journey's end. Mrs Crookes, smiling and pleasant in a flowery summer frock, was standing in the doorway of her house and waved at us to come inside. Vinny, who hadn't altered much except that he had more colour in his cheeks, showed us round his new home.

I had never seen an inside lavatory or a bathroom before, and couldn't believe that you could get hot water by merely turning on a tap. Vinny demonstrated and, blanketed by steam, we heard his mother call, 'Stop playing about, Vincent, come down here, tea's ready.' Down in the dining room, looking out on a sunny garden full of flowers, very different from the view I had in Michael Road of an asphalt yard, dustbins and water closets, the table was laid with a sumptuous

to their new house by tram. As Vinny passed me and Norman he said, 'So long,' and Mrs Crookes gave my mother their new address. I didn't quite know what to say in farewell, so I gave Vinny a minto, my last one and a bit soft because I had been saving it in my pocket for some time.

One Saturday later that summer, Norman and me boarded the tram outside Brunswick Chapel at the bottom of The Moor for a visit to the Crookes' new home. I was familiar with the route up to Highfields because I had been to the library, but from there on it was new territory to me. We rattled down to Heeley repast. A plate of boiled ham, a pork pie cut into pieces, and a dish in which reposed a round of tinned salmon were surrounded by tomatoes and a bowl of cucumber pickled in vinegar. Piles of thinly-cut bread and butter were ready at hand and, on the sideboard, reinforcements of a bowl of trifle and a seed cake stood by.

Vinny's mother told us to sit down and start as Mr Crookes would be late home, so we all tucked in. I had something of everything and, finishing off with a second bowl of trifle, I thought, 'Why can't every day be like this?' Finally, in spite of the good lady's entreaties to have some more, we had to surrender.

Vinny and George walked down to the end of the road to see us off. George had to return home to obey a call of nature, and Norman hurried along in front of me, scared of missing the tram. I said, 'See you again, Vinny.' He said, simply, 'Yes.' I walked away, turned at the corner, looked back to Vinny and waved farewell. The sun lit his fair hair, making it even lighter as he raised his hand in return.

Up on the top deck of the tram, replete with food and invigorated by the country air, somehow I felt sad, as if a happy part of my life was to be taken away from me forever.

Chapter 6
The Crown and the Crooked Cross

*T*HE LAST YEAR or two had been rather upsetting for my mother. I had always felt that she must have some connection with royalty because as a young woman she looked like Queen Alexandra, and I thought she had me christened George because the King of Greece who bore that name was deposed in the year of my birth. Added to the fact that her father's pickle business was in Queen Street, the evidence of some distant royal connection seemed irrefutable. When some big event took place we had the *Daily Sketch* delivered by Mr Beresford, and my mother saved the copies in a neat pile at the bottom of the wardrobe.

The sadness began when Queen Astrid of the Belgians was killed in a motoring accident, to be followed a year after by the death of our King George the Fifth. As if this was not enough to put up with, his successor to the throne, King Edward the Eighth, abdicated. This didn't upset Mam too much as she didn't like Mrs Simpson anyway. I had read about all these events in the *Sketch* and did a pencil drawing of the late King George, which pleased Mam no end.

Then King George the Sixth and Queen Elizabeth were to be crowned in May at Westminster Abbey, which cheered us all up, especially me, for a big Coronation Pageant was arranged to take place on Bramall Lane football ground and I was to be one of the participants. Our section was to be 'Wounded Soldiers of the Great War'. All of us were kitted out in the regulation army hospital uniform of a bright blue tunic and trousers, white shirt, red tie and a khaki peaked cap. We changed into these at home, then assembled in the school hall in

Hermitage Lane at the side of Brunswick Chapel. Albert Moxay, who had never in his life been so well dressed, remarked as he gazed admiringly at his reflection in the glass panelled door, 'Ar cud stan' bein' shot if thi gennus a suit like dis!' His military smartness was somewhat marred by his footwear, which consisted of a pair of football boots three sizes too big for him and with the studs taken out, giving the toes a rakish upturned appearance.

On the Big Day, the football field was crowded with thousands of children and grown-ups dressed to represent every country and period of the British Empire. Round and round we went, inspired by brass bands and the tumultuous applause of a vast crowd of admiring people. It's the soldier's life for me, I thought, especially when a pretty nurse, nearly my age, re-tied my sling and squeezed my good arm to ease the pain of my wounds. To end the proceedings, everybody marched to pre-arranged positions and formed a huge Union Jack. We stood motionless and the crowd was silent as the massed bands played 'God Save the King'. For a few seconds after the last notes had died away, not a sound could be heard. The flags all around the ground hung limply in the calm air and not a sparrow twittered.

Then, suddenly, and quietly at first, a ripple of clapping like the patter of raindrops broke out on Spion Kop. In a trice it increased in volume — on the terrace, back of the goals and even from the cricket pavilion, until the noise was deafening. It went on and on as we marched in contingents round the ground and received an even greater round of applause as our gallant band of wounded warriors saluted before going down the tunnel, where the sound was strangely muffled.

Back at our mustering place we were greeted with the welcome sight of long trestle tables laden with sandwiches, buns and a huge copper urn of steaming tea. At the sight of all this food and drink, discipline broke down and we thundered across the bare-boarded floor in a motley rabble. A strong authoritative voice quelled us immediately: 'Stop, and stand where you are!'

We froze as still as statues, for it was the commanding tones of Mr Barwell, our headmaster and a veteran of the Great War. His next order was for us to line up in single file at the front of the top table, where he was standing. In spite of his stern face, a happy twinkle in his eye was encouraging, and his following words even more so. 'Now, you've all done very well. I am pleased and proud of you. Everyone has been a credit to St Silas. I think that we were the best-turned-out party on the ground and all of you kept in step, that is with the sole exception of Master Moxay who appeared to be somewhat hampered by his boots!' There was a little chuckle at this, but Albert, with his eyes on the food, was unabashed as he licked his lips and used the sleeve of his tunic for a handkerchief. 'Before we start to eat,' continued our Head, 'in honour of this memorable occasion I am going to present you with two souvenirs, which I hope you will keep and cherish for the rest of your lives.' 'I wish he'd get on with it,' I thought, my empty stomach rumbling. He did so, and from under a cloth behind the table he produced a golden tin with a picture of Their Majesties on the lid. Even better was to follow. As he handed each one of us this gift, it was accompanied by a stainless steel pocketknife engraved with the date of the Coronation. We took our places at the table and did battle with the food.

Leaning back for a breather, I opened the box and found that it contained a block of Rowntree's milk chocolate wrapped in silver paper. I thought, as I sampled yet another bun, 'I'll be almost sorry to leave school next year.' Back at home I handed over the chocolate to my mother for safe keeping, then changed out of my uniform into mundane everyday clothes.

I felt a bit flat after my short-lived taste of Army life, even though I had only been a wounded soldier who had never taken part in any battle. Lying on a chair in the living room was last Sunday's *People* and a picture on the front page caught my eye. It was of a tall lad with cropped, flaxen hair. He was clad in a smart military-style shirt and very short leather trousers which showed off to their full his brawny thighs and bulging calves. Round his arm was a cloth band emblazoned with the swastika and he was holding up his hand in a salute. The words underneath the photograph said, 'Thirteen years old Helmut Hegnut from Hamburg in Germany and his family on a Mediterranean cruise with the "Strength through Joy" movement.' It appeared that money was deducted from workers' pay packets and the extra cost was borne by the Nazi government. Helmut, it also stated, was a member of the Hitler Youth in which he received a smart uniform and military training. Although he and I were about the same age, as I compared my pasty, skinny arms and spindly shanks with his splendid sun-bronzed limbs, I felt distinctly disadvantaged. I was also a bit put out because I had only ever had one holiday in my life at the seaside, and that was at Skeggy, and yet here was Helmut off on a sea cruise.

'Dad,' I said, to get Father's attention as he was about to doze off. 'How is it that Jerries can have holidays like this and we don't get any at all?' He moved uneasily in his chair, as he always did when I propounded a difficult question. 'Well Georgie,' he answered, 'it's like this. Over there they've got this feller that used to be a house painter, called Schickelgrüber who nobody took any notice of, then he changed his name to Hitler and everybody falls for what he tells 'em. I suppose we would here if we got holidays like that.' Warming to his theme, he carried on, 'Why, he's even promised every worker a new car called the Volkswagen. I could do with one, I know that — my old van's about had it.' Pursuing my point further, I asked, 'Can't we have summat like the Hitler Youth over here? It sounds a bit more exciting than the Boys Brigade, all they have is a week in a tent at Torksey.' Father picked up the *Telegraph*, which was always a sign that the conversation was about to close. 'We . . . ll,' he said after a little deliberation, 'It's a bit different over here. We've got a bloke in charge called Baldwin who hasn't changed *his* name, but nobody believes a blind word he says. Perhaps it's as well, because all he offers us is higher taxes and lower wages.' Chuckling in spite of himself, he continued, 'Anyway, *we'd* all look well flinging up an arm and shouting "Bravo Baldwin!" every time we met anybody, and I bet you'd feel a bit silly being called a Baldwin Boy, now wouldn't you?' With this gem of parental wisdom, he took refuge behind the *Telegraph* and I with *Oliver Twist*.

Chapter 7
Rejected

AT THE mature age of twelve, one morning at school just as I was leaving to go home for dinner, Mr Beresford called me back to his desk. I returned in some trepidation. What had I done wrong?

However, he gave me a friendly smile, displaying white teeth seldom seen in Headford Street, and said, 'There are some places available at the Technical College in Bow Street, Cunningham.' He paused. I wondered what he was on about, thinking I would be late for my dinner, until he continued. 'It's a very good place to learn a trade. Every pupil is given a thorough training in engineering, both theoretical and practical, until sixteen years of age, with every prospect of getting a decent job.' Again he said nothing for a few seconds, eyeing me quizzically. 'I've put your name down on the list of entrants for the entrance examination in June and I'm sure that with some extra effort you should stand a fair chance of passing.'

Thoughts of what was for dinner vanished from my mind as I tried to digest what Mr Beresford was informing me. 'It will be a great honour for the school as there are only five vacant places at the College and it should be the start of a career in engineering for you.' I gulped nervously, not knowing what to say, although it didn't seem to matter what I thought. Mr Beresford, evidently under the impression that I was too overcome with joy to speak, stood up and told me to go home and tell my parents, adding, 'I'm sure that they will be as delighted as you are by this good news.'

I wasn't all that chuffed as I walked home along Moore Street that momentous dinnertime. Dad and Mam, too, although they made

remarks such as 'You could do a lot worse', didn't appear to be over-joyed, especially Mam, who said, 'You'll have to look after that chest of yours if you go to work in a factory.' All the remaining months of the year, I wrestled with the complexities of arithmetic — most of which was incomprehensible to me — technical drawing, which I rather enjoyed, and grammar, which made me wonder what it had to do with engineering.

The fatal day of destiny dawned and I joined a crowd of budding engineers entering the College premises. The old stone building, with the words 'Central Schools' carved over the doorway, seemed vastly superior to my present seat of learning, St Silas, for which already I felt a pang of yearning. For two days I wrestled with the paperwork in the large well-lit examination room, returning home in the late afternoon with the feeling of being released from boarding school because there hadn't been time to come home for dinner.

On the third day, we were taken into the machine shop where some of the older pupils were working on machines. As soon as I entered, the sickly smell of soluble oil assailed my nostrils, increasing the fear I always had of anything mechanical. The longer I was in contact with them, the worse I got. The sight of lathes spinning so quickly, spewing out glistening turnings, surface grinders sparking away and milling machines grouting away, all accompanied by whirling pulleys and slapping belts, must have made an impression on my features because the instructor, quite kindly, inquired if I felt alright. I nodded, not trusting myself to speak, but stood at the back of the others as far away from the machinery as I could. The older pupils, who looked to me like men, although they were only fifteen or sixteen, clad in blue overalls, with steel rules in the leg pocket, appeared to be enjoying themselves, pressing buttons, turning handles and pulling levers with an air of nonchalance, which I envied.

At the back of the shop, a lathe had been set aside for a demonstration and also the opportunity for engineering tyros to try their hand, under the watchful eye of an instructor. Although I had kept at the back, my turn came all too soon and I found myself standing on the duckboard with the dreaded machine before me. Even though it was motionless, I broke into a sweat, and the palms of my hands and the soles of my feet tingled with fear as the instructor said, 'Right, Cunningham — that's your name, isn't it? — pull this handle which will engage the belt.' This I hesitatingly did, and miraculously the machine sprang into life, startling me so that I stepped back off the duckboard. The instructor, mistaking my fear for inexperience, said 'Steady lad, take your time. I'll show you how to put a cut on.' He expertly twirled two handles, the cutting tool moved quickly to the bar of steel held in the chuck, and, hey presto! a shining sliver of steel curved away. He wound the handles back, stood to one side and told me to do what he had done. The confidence that the starting procedure had given me evaporated quickly as I grasped the handles. Just as the tool was about to contact the steel, a wave of fear came over me and I closed my eyes. There was a grinding sort of thud and a severe jar that shook my arms. I opened my eyes to see the belt coming down off the pulley and the machine stopped dead. The silence that followed was broken by the instructor saying wearily, 'When I said put a cut on, I meant on to the steel. You rammed the tool into the chuck!' Luckily, no damage was done, although my arms tingled a bit and my fear of machines and their duplicity had increased.

When I got home later that day, my father asked me how I had gone on, but thankfully didn't pursue the matter when I replied, 'Alright.' I knew full well it hadn't been so and on the ensuing days I pinned my hopes on the prospect of having failed the entrance exams and continuing my educational career at dear old St Silas.

The days turned into weeks and still no results had come through, increasing my belief that either I hadn't been accepted or the Technical College wished to forget about me after my performance on the lathe. It was not to be. Mr Beresford's and Mr Barwell's jubilant faces greeted me at school and I was informed that I had passed the entrance examination and could enrol at the Technical College at the beginning of term. Mr Beresford took me aside at dinnertime and said enthusiastically, 'This is the start of a new life for you. With the training you will receive a good job will be yours at the end of it, not errand ladding which I am afraid is the most you could have hoped for.' To me, carrying a basket in the open air seemed infinitely preferable to being caged in a factory, surrounded by hellish machinery. 'Give this to your father,' he continued, handing me an envelope. 'It is to inform him of what he has to pay for what you will require at the College.' I was stricken with fear at the thought of spending the rest of my life doing something which I not only disliked, but of which I was terrified. My mother, too, was non-committal when I told her the news, more concerned that I was only pecking at my dinner, rather than wolfing it down as I usually did.

Dad, when he came in from his van, opened the envelope and carefully read the enclosed forms. His expression, which had started off cheerful enough at the news of my acceptance, gradually clouded over with gloom as he finished reading. He looked at Mam and said, 'By gum, they certainly need some stuff to learn engineering. Running shoes, shorts, a uniform, drawing instruments, books and things. I suppose we'll have to manage somehow.' She too looked worried. Although the visits to the pop shop had finished, the pickle business was only just managing to keep going, some weeks better than others, but never with a steady income. I pushed my half-finished dinner aside and said, tremulously, 'I, I don't want to go, Dad.' Although he tried to conceal his relief, in spite of his assertions that he would find the money somehow, it was obvious that my decision was a weight off his mind.

That afternoon, when I told Mr Beresford, he looked at me in sheer disbelief. 'Are you sure that you mean it? Think it over for a few days. You are giving up the chance of a lifetime,' were but a few of the attempts to persuade me to change my mind. All to no avail, I stood my ground, the fear of machinery over-riding all Mr Beresford's cajoling and the promise of a brilliant career.

Later that year a form was pinned to the notice board inviting applications for the entrance examination at the Sheffield School of Art in Arundel Street. It stated that tuition would be given in drawing, painting, sculpture and modelling. This really interested me, and also Moxay, who said, 'Ar fink ar'll 'av a gu at dat. Sumdy towd me dat di spend orl day drawin' women wi nowt on!' I hastened to hand in my name to Mr Beresford, confident that he would accept it as I usually did pretty well in the half-hour allocated to artistic pursuits. He looked steadfastly at me for a few seconds, then leant back in his chair and put the fingers of his hands together, as he often did when about to make an important statement. 'You always do well in the art lesson, Cunningham,' he began. I stood before him, already visions of being an artist forming in my mind. The sunny south of France, picnics in a forest glade with fellow artists and our models were rudely shattered by his next words as he continued. 'If you hadn't let down the school, myself and Mr Barwell, I would have been only too pleased to have forwarded your application, but in view of your rejection of the Technical College, I cannot recommend you for a place at the School of Art, that is all.' I stumbled back to my desk, blinking back the salty chagrin tears. It was small consolation, when during playtime in the school yard, Moxay put his arm around my shoulders and exclaimed, 'Ne'er mind, Jud, owd Pew wunt let me gu, either, 'e said wot 'e'd seen o' my drawins nobody cud teach me owt!'

Chapter 8

Britches, Books and an Interview

I WAS thirteen and rapidly growing taller, but not much heavier. Teddy Crabtree, the school wit, greeted me one morning by shouting, 'Nah den, Pirate!' On me enquiring the reason for this new nickname, he laughingly answered, 'Becus tha's gorrer sunken chest!'

Mrs Garlick, our next-door-but-one neighbour, eyeing my knobbly knees and the long gap between the bottom of my trouser legs and the top of my stockings, remarked to Mam, 'It's about time 'e were britched.' Up The Moor we went to Binns', where a very pleasant gentle-man in a black jacket and pinstripe trousers took one look at me, stroked his chin, pursed his lips, then went over to a rack and selected a pair of thick, navy blue melton cloth long trousers. 'Try these on in the fitting room,' he said. I pulled the curtain to behind me, slipped out of my short trousers and pulled on my first pair of 'long uns'. Turning round to admire myself in the mirror, posing manfully with hands in pockets, I felt a coin in one. It was a bright new penny! Buttoning up the flies, I emerged and said to Mam, 'These are alright.' 'Are you sure?' she said anxiously. 'Yes, course they are,' I replied, the penny already beginning to burn a hole in my pocket.

Next day I swaggered along Michael Road, well aware of my mature status and was pleased to bump into Norman Blackwell and let him into the secret of my newly-found wealth. 'Oh,' he said, 'that bloke at Binns' allus does that, 'e puts a penny into pockets o' trousers thi've 'ad for a long time, 'e knows some mug'll fall for it sooner or later. Ar Albert towd me that years since.' When he was britched a couple of weeks later, though, he admitted to me that he'd tried on a dozen

English properly; the half-hour's grammar lesson was all Greek to me. I hadn't the slightest idea what Mr Beresford meant by nouns and pronouns, synonyms, antonyms, adverbs and adjectives. What I did have was a love for the written word and I devoured any book I could get my hands on.

When I was ten I had joined Highfields library and one of the highlights of my week was the walk up London Road and entry into Paradise. Over the door was an inscription carved in stone that said:

That there should be one man die
ignorant who had capacity for knowledge,
this I call a tragedy were it to happen
more than twenty times in the minute as
by some computations it does.

I set myself the task of learning this, but always when I came out because I was so impatient to get inside. The first pleasure after pushing through the turnstile and showing my library ticket was the smell of books, not musty, but somehow faintly perfumed, attracting me to them like a bee to flowers or a dog to a bone. O! the thrill of opening a book for the first time to discover a new world of wonder. Edgar in Clarence Street had introduced me to Charles Dickens and George Borrow and all around me were some new friends to be met: *Coral Island*, *Lorna Doone*, *Robinson Crusoe*

pairs of trousers with no luck, because he'd been served by a less enterprising salesman.

The day came when my nine years of education at St Silas school ended. I and half a dozen scholars were the sole complement of Standard 8. After all those years of schooling, I could write reasonably well, recite the arithmetic tables up to twelve times, read and understand quite a few books and had a fair idea where the principal countries in the world were situated. On the debit site, I could never grasp even the most elementary principles of algebra, and as for reading music, I might as well have been looking at a page of inkblots. Foreign languages weren't in the curriculum, and anyway I couldn't even speak or write

— which should I choose? I was like a starving peasant invited to a banquet, shovelling the magical word down me by the pageful until I finally made my choice and emerged from an enchanted wonderland into grey, drizzly London Road. My father had always encouraged me to read; in fact he let me have all his newspapers except for the *News of the World*, which he said wouldn't interest me, although it did a few years later. So, on that Friday afternoon that seemed to drag on forever, I waited impatiently to be released from the walls of St Silas.

I hadn't the slightest idea what I wanted to do. Being a van lad appeared quite attractive, until I thought that I would have to learn how to drive, which seemed to me about as difficult as flying to the moon. Mr Barwell, the headmaster, shook each of us by the hand, adding a few words of encouragement which appeared genuine enough. When he came to me, he looked steadfastly into my eyes and said, 'Well Cunningham, I hope you do well, though I think that you will always regret not going to the Technical College. You would have made a much better living in engineering than if you had gone to the College of Art and become an artist.' Later that evening, Dad came home earlier than usual from Kenny McLeod's and told me that a Mr Joel, foreman of the stamp shop at Cooper Brothers in Arundel Street, was looking for a handy lad and I was to go and see him in the morning.

Saturday dawned dull and drizzly. I strolled along Eyre Street, yawning and thinking longingly of the warm bed I had left behind me. Charles Lane at eight in the morning was dark and narrowed in by tall buildings, from whose windows dim lights struggled to pierce the grime. I enquired at the time house for Mr Joel, who came across the yard to meet me. He was a short stocky man, in fact not as tall as I was, but much broader with thick forearms and large hands. He had a kindly face and a twinkle in his eyes, enlivened by steel-rimmed spectacles. A stiff white collar, a black knitted tie, navy blue waistcoat and trousers and a white apron tied halfway up his waist gave him more of the appearance of a barman than a foreman stamper.

'Come on then, lad, I'll show you what's what.' We walked across the big, cobbled yard shrouded in steam from big tanks of boiling water. Mr Joel opened a heavy wooden door and we went down a flight of stone steps into the stamp shop. My first impression was the noise. Only the day before I had left the cloistered calm of the classroom, where the loudest bang had been the dropping of a desk lid. Now, huge drop hammers thudded away, leather belting slapped and presses groaned, all in a loud cacophony that was painful to my ears. I saw Mr Joel's lips moving, but I was unable to hear what he said. He escorted me round the shop, showing me the various processes whereby a strip of plain flat metal was miraculously transformed into a spoon or fork embellished with a fancy pattern.

When I was at school we had been taken to the newly-opened Graves Art Gallery in Surrey Street. Some of the pictures, painted by a man called Godfrey Sykes, fascinated me. They depicted the dignity of labour and the working class. All the men were tall, broad-shouldered and muscular with handsome features, curly hair, white teeth and flashing eyes. The workmen in this stamp shop didn't look a bit like that. They were mostly small, round-shouldered, bald-headed and quite a few of them toothless. One of them, displaying pink gums, gave me a friendly gaping grin as I passed him, and a wink that enhanced the fact that he was cockeyed. Yet they seemed strong enough, moving large sheets of metal and lifting heavy boxes full of spoon blanks with apparent ease. One scrawny individual was wielding a huge sledgehammer, driving in a steel wedge held by his equally scrawny workmate in a pair of tongs. I watched, open-mouthed, not a little scared, as the blows thudded home without cessation. What would happen if he missed? The weight of that hammer would carry him halfway across the shop, I thought. But all was well; the die securely held in the tup, and as the blows ceased Mr Joel nodded his approval, then shouted in my ear, 'We'll go up to the office and see Mr Little about starting you.'

It was a relief to me and my ears to leave the noise and grime of the stamp shop and enter the quiet, carpeted offices. I was left standing alone in a tiny oak-panelled outer room, to await Mr Little, the Company Secretary. On the walls were pictures of the owners of the firm: Mr Joe, Mr Arthur and Mr Tom Cooper, three brothers. I thought they all looked very stern, but perhaps they had to be with all their responsibilities. Mr Little, who was quite a large man, bustled in and sat down heavily on the only chair. He had rather a big nose, which was bridged by a pair of horn-rimmed spectacles, which he kept pushing back with a plump forefinger. His hair was dark, parted down the middle and so well brilliantined it outshone his highly-polished black shoes. What with his dazzling white shirt and sharply-pressed smart grey suit, I was a little overpowered by the contrast between him and my future workmates and became tongue-tied.

However, Mr Little, after perusing the last school report I had brought with me, looked thoughtfully at my skinny frame and said,

not unkindly, 'Well, I don't think that a job in the press shop would suit you, or be of any benefit to the firm.' At first I was rather upset, but at the same time glad because, to be honest, I had been frightened by the machinery and noise down below. 'However,' he continued, folding up my report and handing it back to me, 'Mr Beardsall, our designer, has been enquiring about having someone to assist him, so you start on Monday morning.' I wasn't given the opportunity to accept or decline, as he carried on. 'You'll start work at eight o'clock, three-quarters of an hour for dinner and finish at six, Saturday finish at one o'clock. One week's paid holiday a year. Your wages will be nine shillings for a forty-eight-hour week, with a rise of a shilling a week each birthday until you are twenty-one, at which time the situation will be reviewed.' I mumbled out my thanks as he bustled me to the door, down the stairs and into Arundel Street.

All the way home, I exulted in the delights of this vast sum of money being paid to me every week and of my transition in a few days from a callow school lad to a long-trousered, wage-earning workman.

Chapter 9

Mashings and Buffers

THE FOLLOWING Monday I was up early, a bit apprehensive, but at the same time looking forward to the break from the tedium of school and to the start of my career in industry. I reported at the time house in Charles Lane and the timekeeper gave me my clock number and showed me how to clock in. There was a big clock face with Roman numerals in the centre of a huge ring of numbers. An arm with a pointer at the end had to be swung round and then plunged, and I hoped accurately, into the right number. The time was then punched onto a roll of paper inside the apparatus. This accomplished, I was directed up four flights of stone steps, through a buffing shop and then into the sanctum of Mr Beardsall. He swivelled round off a tall stool to greet me and said, 'Take off your jacket and hang it in the corner.' A tall man in his forties, well built with thinning grey hair, a peculiar blankness in one eye and a slight limp in one leg, he was very friendly and soon put me at ease.

The room was small and cosy, very different from the noisiness of the stamp shop. A gas fire glowed in the hearth, and my heart was gladdened by the sight of book-lined shelves and the big drawing board and the racks of silversmithing tools. My duties, Mr Beardsall explained, would be quite simple at first. I was to be taught silversmithing by him, but a number of other duties would have to be performed as well. First thing in a morning I had to sweep the shop clean and, if the weather was cold, light the gas fire. Then he took me down to the silversmiths' shop on the floor below for my introduction to the gas blowlamps and the art of soldering.

I liked it in the lamp shop, as it was called. The flickering flare of a gas flame in the darkness, which changed with the introduction of air into a powerful jet, appeared miraculous to me. All the silversmiths seemed very old. Tom Oxley was thin, and very tall, with a shiny bald head that showed up in the darkness of the lamp shop like a rising moon. Jack Alsop was fat, not very tall, but very wide, with a gusset in the back of his waistcoat and snuff on the front of it. Mr Cooper was the foreman, although he was no relation to the owners. He always wore, even when working at the bench, a brown trilby hat, grease-stained round the band, a stiff white collar and black tie, and a navy blue suit covered by a white apron. He explained to me that their lad had recently left unexpectedly, tempted by an extra sixpence a week to go and work at Roberts and Belk. Would I, therefore, until they could get another lad, mash tea for them?

With Mr Beardsall's permission granted, I went down to the silversmiths' shop at ten o'clock to receive my instructions as to their various requirements of refreshment. Two men whom I had not met before emerged from dark recesses and gave me their mashings. Arnold Whysall, a little man, very thin, with hair that was also very thin, which he tried to make the most of by plastering long strands of it over the top of his bald head, had tea with no milk or sugar. Ernest Habbijam had all his hair, but no teeth — although I never saw him without a pipe in his mouth — and favoured a mashing of tea, sugar and condensed milk, wrapped in a piece of newspaper. I had to scrape off this mixture with a knife blade into his pint pot and the unavoidable

addition of a little printing ink made for a darker and more fragrant brew. Tom Oxley had cocoa in the afternoon, but his morning draught, which I prepared for him, was a pint pot full of cold water into which I plunged a bar of iron I had made red hot with the blowlamp. The little bits of black scale soon subsided to the bottom of the mug, leaving the water clear. Tom sipped this with no sign of enjoyment, confiding in me, 'When ar wor a little lad, doctor said that ar wor anaemic an' ar 'ad ter 'av sum iron in mi blood, so mi mam, who cudunt affoord fancy medicines, used ter stick poker inter fire, then inter a pint o'watter and mek me sup it all, saying it'll do thi' gud.'

Jack Alsop's tipple, too, was a trifle unusual. With a pot full of hot water I had to go into the pickling shop, which was entirely different to Dad's. Here, large tanks lined with lead and full of acid and boiling water bubbled and steamed sinisterly, filling the air with vapour and sulphurous smells that made me sneeze and my eyes water. I had to be very careful. Jack was most particular and could tell in an instant if his brew wasn't exactly right. Feeling like a sorcerer's apprentice, I carefully took the stopper off a huge glass carboy of vitriolic acid, inserted a length of copper wire, withdrew it, then let no more than three drops of the deadly liquid drop into Jack's pot of water. When he drank it, smacking his lips with relish, he explained to me, 'Ar suffer from a bit o' blood pressure, an' sumdy told mi that a drop or two o' vitriol'd thin it darn.' Whether it thinned down his blood or not, it certainly had no such effect on his ample frame, his wobbly treble chins and the spread of his backside over the three-legged stool he occupied at the end of the shop.

One morning when I was in a hurry, Arnold's mashing wasn't in its usual place on the tray. He was busy soldering in the darkness of the lamp shop and, in reply to my enquiry, shouted back over the roar of the blowlamp, 'It's in mi cooat pocket, 'angin' o'er yonder.' I fished out a screw of paper and emptied the contents into Arnold's pot, took it with the others down to the urn and mashed. When I came back he was just emerging, sweating profusely from his labours in the lamp shop. 'Geeus owd a' that pot!' he cried, 'Arm fair gaggin'.' I stood there as he took a long swig, hoping that he may pay me some compliment, when suddenly his features, which had been alight with the anticipation of a soothing drink, altered dramatically, his nose wrinkled in disgust as with a mighty expellation of air and liquid, he ejected the contents of his mouth onto the shop floor. My amazement turned to amusement as he grabbed the empty screw of paper off the bench, unravelled it and shouted, 'Tha daft young clart 'eead, that's an ounce o' dark shag tha's mashed. Mi' mashing wor in t'other pocket!' His temper didn't improve very much when I humorously suggested that I could dry out his tobacco for him, or failing that, perhaps he might try smoking the tea leaves.

One of my other temporary duties was to provide hot water for the buffer lasses in the next shop to ours. There were three of these young ladies: Doris and Nellie, who were sisters, and Alice. First thing of a Monday morning the trio were a picture worth painting. Their hair was covered by a bright red 'eead rag', a long white calico gown called a 'brat' with red material tucked in the neck extended below the knees, and their legs and the tops of their feet were covered in clean brown paper, tied with string. But sadly, after a few minutes' work, a thick film of buffing muck sullied the brightness of this attire and obscured their pretty faces. They were spoon and fork buffers and worked for Mr Mappin, who buffed the heavier hollowware. He was a stoutly-built gentleman with a big drooping moustache, which, when it became heavily powdered with buffing sand, gave him the appearance of a friendly walrus that had been burrowing on a beach.

Every afternoon at a quarter to six, I took a big iron bucket down four flights of stone stairs and filled it with hot water from an urn in the yard. Back up the steps, trying not to spill any, I left the bucket on a shelf beneath a fragment of looking glass and a towel hanging on a nail in a corner of the buffing shop. This feminine retreat was always demurely called by Alice the 'Ladies' Powder Room'. The only powder I ever saw there was a tin of Vim, which was, as Doris often remarked, 'T' get sum o' thick off.'

Mr Mappin was very partial to snuff. Frequently he would straighten up from the spindle, wipe the sand off his moustache with the back of his hand, then delve into a large box that he kept in a cupboard, take a pinch, then administer it to his nostrils and with two mighty inhalations suck the soothing dust up his nose. The bland expression of satisfaction that always followed this performance intrigued me so much that I lashed out tuppence on a tin of Top Mill. In the privacy of our workshop before Mr Beardsall arrived, I tried a pinch. Copying Mr Mappin, I inhaled with all my might. The pungent particles blew up my nose like a tornado of small hot coals. I was racked with uncontrollable sneezes, my eyes streamed with tears and I gasped for breath until the spasm subsided. 'Whew!'

Later that day, when I brought up the water and Mr Mappin had put on his coat, I proffered to him my open, nearly full, tin of snuff. He took his time before accepting and I wondered why he was pinching one of his jacket buttons between a large fleshy thumb and forefinger. I wasn't long in finding out: the indentations in his digits acted like a pair of sugar tongs, and he almost emptied the box as he excavated a quantity of my snuff as big as a walnut. Before applying it to his nose, he held it up for my inspection and gravely informed me, 'That'll teach thee not to act like a mester 'til thar t'owd enuff t'be one!'

46

Chapter 10
The Young Cellini

Geo. Cunningham

IN SPITE of these duties, my silversmithing career blossomed. Mr Beardsall, whose own apprenticeship had been interrupted by the Great War when he joined the Royal Engineers at the age of seventeen, was kindness itself. He had been badly wounded and also lost the sight of one eye in the Battle of Ypres, but his skills were unimpaired. Under his tutorship I learnt the art of soldering and hammering, starting off by making napkin rings in sterling silver. I was also entered by the firm into the silversmithing class at the School of Art in Arundel Street. Mr Bennett, the teacher, was a tall, thin, slightly stooped man, who wore an artist's smock and came from London, so that at first he was rather difficult to understand. The workshops at the College were high-ceilinged and airy, and much better equipped than those at Cooper Brothers. My classmates, whose ages ranged from fourteen to eighteen, were, like myself, all from the many silver firms that abounded in the area. Ted Harding and Edwin Hart were the oldest, and both had a superior air about them, having been at the College longest and also because they worked at Walker and Hall's, the largest silver firm in Sheffield. Our teacher was a complete all-rounder, and in a few months I had learnt the rudiments of hand-raising metal, engraving, and even a little enamelling. I made a child's bowl and drinking mug by hand out of copper and engraved them with pictures of animals and birds, each one named, so that the infant could be taught to read whilst eating.

When I had finished them and they were silver-plated and polished, I entered them, with all the other pupils' work, into the competition of the Worshipful Company of Goldsmiths. To my surprise and delight, they won an award and favourable comment. I had my photo in the *Telegraph and Star* and started work on a plate to complete the child's set. So in 1939, not yet fifteen years old, I felt that I was well on the way to becoming England's Benvenuto Cellini, whose life I had been reading. The grey skies, smoking chimneys and wet cobbled streets of Sheffield were transformed into the sunlit piazzas of the Florence of 'Owd Ben', as I had got into the habit of referring to him, when expounding my knowledge and recently-acquired skills to Norman.

He too had started work, following in his father's footsteps as a turner, and like him he wore a blue boiler suit with the leg bottoms turned up and smelled of soluble oil.

All in all, not a bad year. Dad's pickle business was doing better since he had joined forces with a Mr Frederick Fowler, who, displaying more business acumen than my father, had obtained a bank loan and acquired a factory in Miller Road, Abbeydale. But Dad was not altogether happy. Always an avid newspaper reader, he relied heavily on the predictions in the horoscopes of Lindoe in *The People*. If Dad's stars were favourable, he would be in a good humour, even if most of the front pages seemed to be taken up by Hitler's attempts to take over Europe. Twice a week, I went to the Star or the Landsdowne Picture Palaces and the newsreels had showed the masses of men, tanks and planes moving remorselessly into Austria and Czechoslovakia. In spite of all these ominous sabre rattlings, my father was absolutely convinced that there would be no war because, as he remarked to me over the Sunday breakfast table, 'Lindoe knows what he's talking about, and if he says that there isn't going to be a war, there won't be!' He passed the newspaper over to me, indicating with his finger where the astrologer, in his summing up, prophesied that there would be a peaceful solution to the European crisis. Blithely ignoring this statement, if indeed he had bothered to read it at all, Adolf carried on regardless with his conquests.

Mr Chamberlain, whose position on the international stage carried a little more clout than the stargazer, seemed powerless, even though he had flown back from Munich with a scrap of paper signed by Hitler, assuring us that he only wanted to be friendly and all he asked for was a little more Lebensraum. Having read a lot about the Great War and seen *All Quiet on the Western Front* at the Star Picture Palace, I felt vaguely excited at the prospect of war. After all, we always won and I imagined it to be a series of bayonet charges led always by a dashing young lieutenant in a smart uniform, brandishing his Service revolver, urging his gallant men on to certain victory. In the *War Illustrated* there were loads of pictures like this, and one incident in particular thrilled me to bits. It described how a Captain Nevill, Company Commander of the 8th East Surrey Regiment, on his last leave in London prior to the Battle of the Somme, bought four leather footballs. In the trenches, before the order to fix bayonets and go over the top, he offered a prize to the platoon that first kicked a football up to the German front line. This was his idea of convincing the men that there would be little danger. In fact, as the generals had said, 'It will be a walkover.' The whistles blew and the first kick sailed well in the air, to be followed on the ground by the Captain and his gallant troops. Unfortunately for them, the Jerries, having been shelled for days, were not in a sporting mood that morning, and they immediately shot down Captain Nevill, along with most of his men. Two of the footballs, however, survived the battle and were brought back to England and proudly displayed in a museum.

The expectation of war started to take on the appearance of reality when workmen started digging trenches in the big field at Endcliffe, to be roofed over and used as air raid shelters. Gas masks were issued for everyone, even tiny babies. Cellars were reinforced and Anderson shelters delivered by railway horse and dray, to be erected in back yards or garden, if you had one. Our football and cricket games in the evenings and weekends were postponed and the filling and stacking of sandbags took their place.

Norman Blackwell and me helped Frank Parkin and his father, an ex-soldier, dig a square hole and fix up the corrugated iron sheets of an Anderson shelter in the corner of their yard. One of the sheets fell across my wrist, cutting it rather badly, but I bore up bravely, counting it as my first war wound. Mr Parkin patted the last sandbag into place with the back of a spade, sang a few verses of 'Tipperary', paused for a breather and said, 'Come on, let's have a game of cricket. We can use 'door o' shelter for stumps.' A bat and ball were procured from Norman's house, their Albert joined in and we batted on until bad light stopped play. Rolls of brown paper tape were issued by the ARP and I spent an enjoyable Saturday afternoon pasting this in a trellis-like pattern on all our windows. This, we were told, was to prevent pieces of glass flying about in the event of a bomb blast. My mother wasn't very keen on my efforts, because it was difficult to clean the windows, and, worse still, the tape obscured her view of the goings-on in the street. I don't think that I consoled her very much by saying, 'Well, at nighttime you won't be able to see it behind the blackout blind.'

Chapter 11

Grounded

ALTHOUGH I enjoyed reading these flowing accounts of the British Army's triumphs on the battlefield, I rather fancied joining the Air Force, but at the age of fourteen and a bit I was too young to fly a Spitfire, so I decided to join the Air Training Corps. On presenting myself one Saturday afternoon at the recruiting office, I gave my age, name and address to the smart young man seated at a desk, and was told to go upstairs and wait in a room on the first floor.

I stood there, with a few other hopeful aviators, waiting for something to happen. A clock on the wall ticked the seconds away and only a few nervous coughs broke the silence. Finally, the door opened and a tall distinguished-looking man, in a long white coat with a stethoscope hanging from the pocket, came in and told us to take off our clothes and leave them against the wall.

We were then lined up facing each other so that the doctor could move between us to perform his examination. It didn't take him very long: a look in the mouth, a quick check with his fingers and stethoscope on the chest, and an even quicker check-up on the testicles, seemed all that was necessary, and then we were weighed. As I was waiting my turn, shivering a little in the cold room but trying to stand to attention, I looked at the lad in front of me. I felt definitely superior to him because he was much shorter than me and quite bow-legged. He must have had a dirty job because his legs were quite black, only relieved by rivulets of piss. I sniffed disparagingly, thinking that he'd make a better jockey than a fighter ace.

We lined up again and the doctor came down the ranks, tapping each lad in turn, and saying 'A1', until he came to me and I was told to stand in a corner of the room. I felt quite important; perhaps the ATC had got wind of my prowess as a silversmith or I had been selected for special training for some élite wing in the Royal Air Force. The officer addressed all the rest. 'Well done lads, you've all passed A1. Now get dressed, you'll be hearing from us shortly.' They all looked delighted, especially the jockey, as he struggled to pull up his trousers over his bandy legs.

As the door closed behind the last one, the doctor came over to me and said, 'I didn't want to tell you in front of all the others.' I thought, this is it: Top Secret! 'But,' he continued, 'I have had to fail you. Your height is six feet two inches, but your weight is only nine stones and there is evidence of some lung damage, which may or may not clear up, but we cannot take any chances, so I must declare you C3. I'm very sorry.' I walked slowly over to my solitary pile of clothes. My dreams of being clad in smart RAF blue shattered as I climbed into my workaday melton trousers and pulled the braces over my shoulders — a distinguished career as a fighter ace finished before I had a chance to get off the ground.

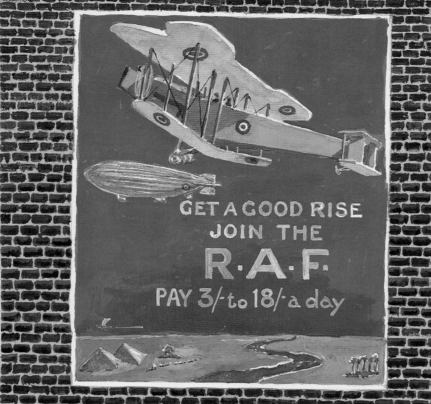

Chapter 12

Happy Birthday

AT THE END of July, Cooper Brothers and Son broke up for a week's holiday. This was a bit of a blow to me, accustomed as I was to a month off from school. The days passed all too quickly. A couple of times Norman, who was also on holiday, and me walked up to Enc's to watch the men sandbagging the air raid shelters. What a contrast to the years before, when we played endless games of cricket on sun-baked pitches surrounded by lush grass. Now heaps of damp-smelling clay, piles of sand and sacks littered the field. The shelters were dug as trenches, with the sides and top reinforced with sheets of corrugated iron, then covered over with sandbags. Anyone could join in, and soon gangs of kids, youths and men were helping with the work. A scuffle broke out between two lads as to whose turn it was to use the shovel. It developed into a rolling wrestling match which was broken up by one of the workmen who pulled the pair apart and held them at arm's length, telling them, 'If you want to' fight, gu and join 'army an' tek it art on 'bloody Jerries. There's plenty o' them t' 'ave a gu at!' Indeed there was. I went to the Star Picture Palace one evening and the newsreel was taken up almost entirely with pictures of huge rallies in Germany, with hundreds of thousands of Nazis in tremendous torch-lit rallies, which made our Coronation Day turn-out look a bit sparse, to say the least.

My father still had faith in Lindoe's prediction that peace would pre-vail, but Adolf, with his celebrated instinct for fair play and keeping a straight bat, claimed that Poland had attacked the Third Reich and, his patience being exhausted, what else could he do but retaliate? Ignorant though I was of international strategies, the idea of Poland having a go at Adolf's lot was rather like me assaulting Joe Louis.

To prove that his quest for a peaceful settlement was sincere, the Führer ordered the Luftwaffe to strafe Warsaw and Cracow, battleships to bombard Polish ports, and his tanks to cross the frontier. Mr Chamberlain, according to the wireless that I had taken to listening to more frequently, was very upset by this rather forceful method of peacemaking, and asked Mussolini, who was a bosom pal of Adolf's, to say that Britain was still willing to negotiate if German troops were withdrawn. Hitler, with the ball at his feet and confident that he could have the war over and won in a couple of weeks at the outside, politely rejected the proposal and went on with his attempts to establish peace by increasing the intensity of his attacks on defenceless people.

Sunday the 3rd of September 1939 dawned bright and clear, and it was my fifteenth birthday. I came down to breakfast, rather late. My brother had already gone out, leaving Dad in possession of the table, and Mam was in the kitchen. The wireless was on and a cloth had been thrown over Charlie the canary's cage so that his chirping wouldn't interfere with the broadcast, which said that an ultimatum had been delivered to Berlin. There was nothing more and I thought, 'This is a bit tame. Why don't we have a go at Germany? Adolf doesn't play to the whistle, why should we?'

I finished breakfast — always a good fry-up on a Sunday, now that trade was picking up in the pickle business — put on my jacket and said, 'I'm popping round to Norman's, and then we might go for a walk.' My mother's face was strained and anxious, with the hint of a tear, as she said, 'Don't go too far, we don't know what's going to happen.' Outside, Michael Road was quiet and sunny — even Wells' coconut-matting dog wasn't out — the sky was blue and sunshine glinted on the silver barrage balloons. I took my gas mask in its cardboard box, on which I had inscribed a rather colourful monogram of my initials, and walked up the entry into Norman's back yard.

Knowing his usual Sunday morning programme, I didn't go to the Blackwell residence, but crossed over the yard to the row of lavatories. The door of the third one was ajar and from behind it Norman's voice, slightly strained, bade me ''Ow do, Georgie, ar'll not be long. Many 'appy returns.' A sound of newspaper being ripped off a nail, followed by a thunderous rush of water, heralded the appearance of Norman, pulling braces over his shoulders and looking relieved as he locked the door. It didn't take him long to complete his toilet: a quick rinse of the hands, which he dried by smoothing down his hair, and we were off. For some time now, our Sunday morning pastime had been a walk up one side of The Moor and then back down the other. Somehow, this particular Sunday seemed strangely different; apart from the odd tram, there was little traffic and only a few people.

We were on the return trip, passing the Central Picture Palace, and I was trying to decide whether to lash out on two pints of sarsaparilla to celebrate my birthday, or say nothing and have a bottle of burdock to myself. Suddenly, a man dressed in an oil-stained boiler suit and heavy boots rushed out of Earl Street and shouted to no one in particular, 'Thi's a waar on,' then disappeared as quickly as he had come. Norman and I, and one or two passers-by, gazed blankly at each other, then with one accord we all looked up at the sky. It was still there, reassuringly calm and blue. The only things flying were a few pigeons, which had been startled by the announcement. Norman, as ever the realist, exclaimed, 'We'd better gerrooam an' 'av us dinner befoor 'e starts droppin' 'em.' We trailed down The Moor and up Clarence Street. Everywhere was very quiet, not even a shop window gazer or a tab-end collector in sight. A bit of a let-down, I thought, having visualised masses of troops and tanks rushing to the coast to defend England.

Back home my mother was preparing dinner: always on a Sunday a half-shoulder of lamb from Gledstone's the butcher. She was indeed very worried. My brother was seventeen and I was fifteen, so unless

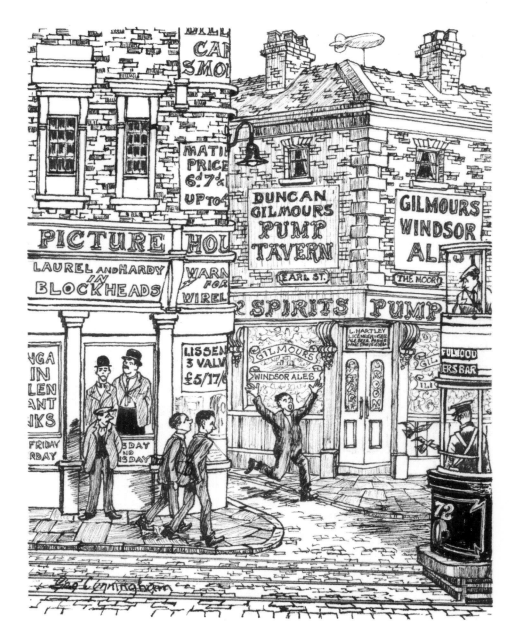

the war was over very soon we could possibly share the same fate as many of her girlhood friends had done in the Great War. Father, too, was upset. Lindoe had let him down and he had missed his usual Sunday morning tram ride to Millhouses and a couple of pints in the Wagon and Horses. He kept trying to read the paper, but all the time he was glancing at the clock and checking his watch. Finally he stood up and declared, 'I'll just go up and have one at Sam's, I'll not be long.' Donning his trilby, without which he never ventured outdoors, we set off, assuring mother that if anything happened we would come straight home. Up to now my fifteenth birthday hadn't been all that exciting, so I left my father outside the Devonshire Arms, presided over by the legendary Sam Palfreyman, and crossed over the road to the drink shop to have a little celebration.

To my surprise, Harry Flathers, whom I had not seen since my schooldays, greeted me from his position near the counter. 'Nar den, Jud, ar tha guin' on?' followed up by the query, 'Can tha lend me threpence fer a pint? Ar've cum art wiart mi money.'

I did as he requested and ordered a pint of sass for myself, wondering at the same time what Flathers was doing in a drink shop if he had no money. Taking a generous slurp of the dark potent brew, he leaned over so that his mouth was close to my ear and whispered hoarsely and confidentially, 'Mi fadder's doing a little job round corner an' 'e told me ter wait 'ere forrim.' Harry's appearance hadn't improved since he left school. He was taller and thinner, and even his nose seemed to have grown longer, as had his legs, for his trousers were at half-mast, the turn-ups ending at his calves. He seemed to be living well enough though. Mingling with the aroma of sass I could distinctly smell dripping; as I averted my face from Flathers, I could clearly discern the fatty evidence, sprinkled with breadcrumbs around his mouth. The sarsaparilla didn't seem to be having a soothing effect on him, as he was continually glancing over the top of the window

curtain. Then, suddenly emptying his pot in one tremendous gulp, he gasped, 'Ar'll si thi,' and dashed out of the shop.

Startled as I was by this unseemly behaviour, I went to the door and observed Flathers Senior with a sack over his shoulder running up Ecclesall Road, hotly pursued by a portly policeman. I gaped, open-mouthed, amazed by the spectacle, but Harry's reaction was instantaneous. The pint pot, which he had conveniently forgotten to replace on the counter, was flung with unerring aim through the window of John Thomas Cufflin's barber's shop. The constable, hearing the tremendous crash, skidded to a halt, turned, but could see nothing because Harry had dived down Renton Street. By the time the arm of the law could resume the chase, his original quarry had also disappeared. Sweating profusely in his thick uniform, and hampered by a military gas mask and tin hat, the policeman gave it up as a bad job, plodded back to Cufflin's, took out his notebook and jotted down a description of the damage. I went back into the shop and sat down on one of the wooden forms. The proprietor, Mr Oates, emerged from his living room, picking something out of a tooth. 'What were that bang? Ar thought it wor Jerries.' I realised I had better keep quiet, having been the sole witness to a heinous crime, so I merely remarked that it was a car that had backfired.

Sitting in the gloom of the drink shop in that September morn, I cogitated about my future. What would be my role in the war? Failed by the ATC, overgrown and underweight and liable to a racking cough, my only skill a year's silversmithing, I thought that the ability to make a child's set wouldn't help the war effort, or deter the Germans. Just when I was on the point of drinking up and leaving, the door opened and Albert Moxay made a dramatic entrance by tripping over the doorstep. Since we left school, our meetings had been infrequent and he had grown quite a bit taller and put on some weight. He still sported a tidemark around the neck, but his wrists were covered by jacket sleeves which came down to his fingertips. The trousers he wore were braced up so tightly that the waist band was nearly up to his armpits. I had never seen Moxay in a suit, except on Coronation Day, and he tried to appear unaffected by his sartorial elegance by putting his hands in the trousers pockets, but they were so high that he contented himself by grasping the lapels of his jacket. 'Not a bad fit, eh? Mi fadder got called up last week, an afoor 'e went 'e said ar cud wear his suit on Sundays, s' long as ar looked after it.'

The meeting with Moxay cheered me up, especially when he treated me to a pint of sass, flashing a handful of silver like the man who broke the bank at Monte Carlo. He told me that he had got a job, but as it was war work he 'had to keep it dark', winking knowingly at me, and at the same time laying a dirty forefinger down the side of his nose, as if to imply that I was to enquire no further. However, as he got down his pint and the wine flowed in and the wit flew out, he ordered a bar of Cadbury's chocolate, broke two squares off for me and, gulping down the rest, mumbled, 'Ar'm on a good thing. Just round corner from us, a builder purrup some wooden scaffoldin' and battens, ready to start next day, but sum ar 'em found their way inter ar cellar!' Moxay chuckled with glee at my mystified expression. 'Naow, soft sod, ar'm not guing to start building, ar'm sawing poles in bits, then chopping 'em up fer firewood, an' selling 'em at tuppence a bundle!' I felt a bit miffed that I hadn't thought of anything like that, and even more so when the young entrepreneur declared that he would easily make a quid on the first lot and that he already had his eye on some more.

It was getting on for dinnertime, so I walked along Moore Street with Moxay and bade him farewell at the corner of Clarence Street. The Sunday somnolence was unbroken; there seemed to be an uncanny calm, as if everyone was indoors waiting for something to happen. My father arrived home shortly after me, and then my brother Bill.

It was a fine, warm day and the room was hot from the fire and hotter still when my mother opened the oven door to take out the joint.

She and Dad had a glass of beer apiece and Bill and me a burdock before the meal was dished up. Dad was in good spirits. He seemed to have got over the let-down by Lindoe, and, with the help of Ward's fine malt and his pals in the Devonshire, had made an assessment of the war situation. 'Fred Clayton,' he began, 'says we've nothing to worry about being bombed. Sheffield's surrounded by seven hills and the Germans will never find us.' To amplify this statement, he carried on, 'Fred says there's only one other city in the world with seven hills, and that's Rome.' Finishing on this cheering statement, he took a drink of beer and commenced carving. As I waited for my plate to be filled, I wondered why it was that Fred Clayton, who was the cobbler next door to the Devonshire Arms, knew this and the British Government didn't. I thought that if he had told them this a couple of years ago it would have saved all the time and money building air raid shelters, training ARP workers, flying barrage balloons, and my mother the irritation of having her windows taped up. Dinner over, Bill went out, Mam started washing the pots and Dad settled down in the armchair to read the *News of the World*.

In a few minutes, his head was on his chest and the paper was strewn all over the floor. I picked them up and a phrase caught my eye: 'Intimacy took place'. I was about to read on when Dad stirred, but before I could ask him what it meant, he was snoring.

The afternoon dragged on. I went and had a chat with Norman, standing in the entry, though the day was sunny. 'Mi dad's not bothered about Hitler. He says war'll gi 'im plenty o' work, 'im bein' a turner 'n me learnin' to be one, thi'll be bags of o'ertime.' I didn't like to damp his enthusiasm by suggesting a fat pay packet would not be much protection against a bomb.

The evening came. The wireless news was all about the German advance and the heroic resistance of the Poles, some of whom were even making cavalry charges against the enemy tanks. Unusual for Dad, he didn't go down to the Royal Oak, and then at ten o'clock he wound his watch, checked the blackout blinds, raked out the fire, covered the cage of Charlie the canary and we all went to bed. I was soon asleep, though my rest was disturbed by vivid dreams. At one time I was with Moxay, charging at the Germans with a scaffold pole, and the next minute back at school, fighting with Jackie Wrathfull. He was shaking me, and with all my might I was trying to fend him off. The dreams turned into reality. It was Dad who had hold of me and was crying, 'Come on, get up, the sirens are going!' Indeed they were. I had heard them on practices, but then they only sounded the 'all clear' to make sure that people could hear them. This was the real thing — an uncanny moaning sound that would chill the blood in daytime, never mind dead of night.

Bill and me scrambled out of bed. I started pulling my trousers over my pyjamas and got both feet down one leg; my braces were in a tangle and so was I. All I could think of was getting downstairs, which I did eventually. Down in the living room, Dad, Mam, Bill and me donned our gas masks with trembling fingers, then stood there looking at each other. We all looked alike: ugly. 'What do we do now?' None of us had any idea. We had no air raid shelter, Garlick's cellar wasn't ready, the Germans could soon be dropping

bombs, gas and incendiaries on our defenceless heads, and all we could do was stand there and wait.

Suddenly Dad had an idea. 'We'll go to Pickering's. Ernest Garlick says they've got big deep cellars and that's where he's going if there's a raid.' We cautiously emerged into Michael Road. All was quiet and very dark in the blacked-out street, then there was a shuffling of feet and voices as people emerged from entries. At first the pace was slow, then someone broke into a trot. Everybody followed suit, even older people, until we arrived at the big wooden doors of the factory. Mr Blackwell, Norman's father, started banging on the small wicket gate with one hand, holding up his trousers with the other. There was a babble of voices, muffled by our gas masks, and more of the leaders began banging on the doors. Suddenly there was a click, the rattle of a bolt, the wicket door opened inwards and standing there was the resolute figure of Mr Anthony, the caretaker of Pickering's cardboard box factory. He wore a long dark blue overcoat and an ARP steel helmet, a military gas mask, and in one hand held a thick walking stick and in the other a large flash lamp.

At the sight of him the babble ceased. Mr Blackwell and the rest stopped banging. Sounds emerged from behind Mr Anthony's gas mask, then realising he couldn't be heard he took it off, revealing a hot flushed face, stamped with authority and tinged with irritation. 'What's all the noise about?' he demanded. Mr Blackwell tore off his gas mask to reply. 'Cum on den, lerrus inter cellar, 'e'll be droppin' 'em soon.' This request was backed up vociferously by the crowd, and for a moment it looked as though we would storm the gates and occupy the firm by force. Mr Anthony, though, was built of sterner stuff. He held up his torch like a mace bearer, and proclaimed, 'I cannot allow anyone on these premises, night or day, without written authorisation from Mr Truelove.'

Albert Blackwell, maskless and toothless, looked at him with stunned disbelief. 'Tha wot?' he gasped. 'Mester Truelove lives in Psalter Lane. Dusta think Jerries ar gunna wait 'til sumdy runs up theer an' back?' Not to be moved, the guardian of the factory stood his ground and said, 'It's more than my job's worth to let anybody in without a permit.' From the crowd angry rubbery mumblings became louder, then suddenly, from the back, a woman's high-pitched voice screeched, 'Shuv 'im arter rooad, Albert, wisel all gerrus deeath o' cowd standin' art 'ere!'

With the twin fears of death by bombing and pneumonia, there was a surge towards the gates. Mr Anthony tried to close the wicket gate, but Albert had his foot in it. For a long desperate moment, it looked as if the custodian would be overcome, then all at once a blessed sound rent the air. No heavenly trumpet ever sounded sweeter than did that first all clear of the war. On and on it went, but it could never be monotonous because it meant safety and freedom from fear, at least for the time being. As the last note faded away, sighs of relief and one or two 'hurrays' broke the silence, followed by a babble of conversation and the crying of children as we all took off our gas masks. Mr Anthony said farewell by banging and bolting the wicket gate, confident that he had done his duty. Back along Michael Road we straggled. I thought how different people looked from the day before. None of the men had collars and ties on; Albert Blackwell's shirt lap was hanging out; all the women's hair was untidy and quite a few hadn't had time to put in their false teeth. At each entry people wished each other good night, a little self-consciously. Our family lingered for a minute at Blackwell's entry. Mr Blackwell had regained his composure and his appearance, having finally untangled his braces and put in his false teeth which he produced from his pocket remarking, 'Ar purrem in theer in case ar got mi 'eead blown off. Arve ony just gorrem and ar din't want to gerrem brocken.' He was quite a small man, though in my eyes his stature had increased considerably by his determined assault on the factory door. 'Warra weekend,' he expostulated, 'Wot wi Wednesday gerrin' licked yesterday at 'ooam bi Plymouth, 'n Jerries keepin' us up hafe art neet, ar'll be glad ter get back t' work.' From the darkness of the entry he said, 'G'night, Sid,' which to me was an unaccustomed familiarity because he had always addressed my father as 'Mr Cunningham'.

I was glad to get back to the peacefulness of our house, climb into the still warm bed and lay there, while thinking what an eventful fifteenth birthday I'd had, and wondering how many more I would live to see.

Chapter 13

The Phoney War

THE TREMENDOUS events overseas had little impact at home. Joe Stalin stepped in with his two penn'orth and took half of Poland and then, for an encore, had a go at Finland. Adolf ordered his fat friend, Herman Göring, to prepare for a five years' war and the Graf Spee scuttled herself in faraway Montevideo.

As 1939 faded away and the long-awaited spring of 1940 shortened the nights, I began to think that Fred Clayton, the cobbler-strategist, may have been right. All we had were one or two false air raid alarms. At Cooper Brothers virtually nothing had changed. Apart from a few gross of NAAFI spoons and forks, the production was just the same as it had been prior to hostilities commencing. I thought that we would have changed immediately to something exciting, like making guns and bombs, or plane parts, or even bayonets.

All that did happen was that Mr Beardsall designed, on the instructions of Mr Joe Cooper, a tea and sugar container. This contribution to the war effort was a small round tube about four inches long, divided in the middle by a partition and capped at each end. Made of sterling silver, beautifully engine-turned, with a shield left bare for the owner's monogram, it was a must for wealthy people to take their own tea and sugar rations when visiting friends. It was in sharp contrast to the newspaper-clad mashings I was still doing for the silversmiths, and as I hammered and soldered these silver war winners, I wondered what Hitler would think about our secret weapons.

So the phoney war continued, and my father and the rest of the alehouse war cabinet held regular sessions in Kenny McLeod's, the Devonshire Arms and the Wagon and Horses at Millhouses. It seemed to be stalemate on the Western Front, and apart from a trifling incident like invading Norway in April, the Jerries appeared to be content to sit out the war behind their Siegfried Line, even though as the popular song had it, we were going to use it to hang out our washing. Dad said, when he arrived home from a particularly informative high-level meeting, 'Old Fred says it'll be nothing like the last lot. The Germans don't want another pasting, and anyway, sez Fred, they'll never get through the Maginot Line.' Before the war a lot of newspapers had articles and photographs of this wonderful achievement. I read them avidly, fascinated that hundreds of thousands of highly-trained crack soldiers could be deep underground in bomb- and shell-proof quarters, from which railway trains could rush them to thwart any German attack. Heavy artillery, unseen from ground level, could be raised up on hydraulic lifts and even tanks could be brought into action. Coupled with the fact that hundreds of miles of barbed wire, minefields and tank traps were also all along the French frontier with Germany, it was an impregnable barrier.

Whilst we were waiting for Sunday dinner to be served, Dad poured himself a glass of beer and said, complacently, 'I was talking to Ernest Garlick. He was in the last lot and he sez Hitler'll have to pack it in. He'll never get through that Maginot Line in a hundred years!' Mr Garlick, who lived next door but one to us, was a wiredrawer by trade, which in my opinion didn't exactly qualify him to be an expert on military strategy, but as the phoney war dragged on, his prophecy

Geo. Cunningham

appeared to be correct. Adolf, however, who wasn't noted for fair play or observing Queensbury rules, didn't attack the unassailable defences head-on, but instead ordered his armies and panzers to take sharp left- and right-handers through neutral Holland and Belgium and emerge, practically unscathed, behind the Maginot Line. In a very few weeks the Nazis had occupied Paris. The *Daily Sketch* had a photo on its front page that caught my eye. It showed German troops marching down the Champs Elysées, and I would have bet my last minto that in the foreground was Helmut Hegnut from Hamburg.

Even though Jerry soon reached the French coast and we had to evacuate the BEF from Dunkirk, the mood in England — well anyway in Sheffield — was that: 'Alright, Adolf's won first round, but just wait 'til we get our breath back, then we'll show him!'

Things were getting crucial, too, at Cooper Brothers. The supply of sterling silver had dried up and I had to resort to making the tea and sugar containers out of an inferior metal, known in the trade as German Silver, which struck me as being rather ironic in the light of the current situation. I continued with my classes at the School of Art and did a drawing of a plate to complete the child's set. When it was done to Mr Bennett's satisfaction, a circle of copper was procured and I hand-hammered

it into shape. Even though I was only sixteen, I was quite adept with the blowlamp and the dozens of hammers and various tools of the silversmithing craft. There was something

Geo. Cunningham

very satisfying in hammering a flat sheet of metal and hopefully seeing it turn into a thing of beauty and a joy forever.

Chapter 14
Bombs and a Bird

*T*HE AUTUMN faded into winter and on a cold frosty evening in December, feeling a bit flush with money as I had received a shilling a week rise on my birthday, Bill and me decided to go to the first house at the Landsdowne Picture Palace. It was Thursday, one of the nights I should have attended the School of Art, but I eased the pricks of conscience by telling myself that the child's plate only needed engraving to finish, and that process I could easily do before end of term.

The old 'Lanny' was pretty full when we took our seats in the sixpennies, just in time for the start of the programme. A Three Stooges film was on first, with Curly, Larry and Mo in cracking form, and then came the newsreel. Hitler had apparently decided to switch his peacemaking bombing overtures from London to give Liverpool and Coventry a sample of his benevolence. As scenes of devastation and death flickered on the screen, a flat-capped Jonah at the side of me muttered to his headscarfed wife, 'It'll be ar turn next, just thee see.' I sniffed contemptuously at this ill-informed remark. Evidently he was unaware of Fred Clayton's seven hills that shielded Sheffield from the Luftwaffe. The prediction of the cobbler had been proved correct a fortnight earlier, when hundreds of German planes flew over Sheffield on their way to Liverpool, without dropping a bomb, and Dad said, 'Fred's right, they can't find Sheffield.'

It was with some surprise, then, that halfway through the big picture, a boring film about nursing called *Vigil on the Night* starring Carole Lombard and Brian Aherne, a message of war flashed on the screen,

informing us that the air raid sirens had sounded. This was followed by an announcement from the manager that the show would go on. There had been so many false alarms during the past weeks that only a few people got up and left the cinema. Most of the audience stayed on, not because it was a particularly entertaining film, but having paid a tanner we were determined to get our money's worth. At quarter-past eight, *Vigil on the Night* thankfully ended. 'God Save the King' was played and we all filed out.

In the foyer stood the commissionaire, nicknamed 'Bulldog' because his undershot lower jaw and big eyeteeth bestowed on him a distinct likeness to our national symbol. Being an old soldier he was quite calm when he growled 'Gerrof 'ooam quick as y' can, 'ee's droppin' 'em.' Out in London Road all was quiet in the moonlight. A few searchlights roamed the heavens. There was a rosy glow down near St Mary's Church and an acrid smell of burning in the air, very different from the ever-present aroma of coal fires. Bill and I sauntered along, laughing about the antics of the Three Stooges, and we had just crossed over Cemetery Road when a noise like an express train travelling at high speed rent the air. A tremendous thump on the ground lifted me off my feet, and when I landed back on them I was off alongside my brother, like a pair of sprinters. Another almighty 'Crump!'

was followed by what sounded like a shower of tin cans falling on the slates. 'Incendiaries,' gasped Bill, as we tore up Clarence Street and into our back yard. I didn't knock on Mrs Garlick's door. We went straight into the house, stumbling against the furniture in the darkness of the living room and clattered down the spotless, donkey-stoned steps into the cellar. It had been reinforced with corrugated

sheeting to provide an air raid shelter for the four families in the yard.

Anxious faces stared at us as we ducked under the low doorway. My mother cried out, 'Where have you been all this time? We've been down here ages — it's terrible!' Although she meant well, a tightening of lips and a direct look from Mrs Garlick indicated that she had taken it as a personal slight against her cellar, which like the rest of the house was a credit to her. The corrugated sheeting was whitewashed, and the supporting pillars painted a pleasant green. Even the floor was carpeted, complete with a pegged rug. A single bulb in a pretty shade gave just enough light for us to see each other. From the corner nearest to the gas meter a racking cough indicated the presence of Mrs Hill from the bottom house. Mr and Mrs Garlick and their family, Joyce, Betty, Gordon and Nigel, sat all together on a long wooden form. Mrs Taylor, their next-door neighbour, her husband being a window cleaner and used to climbing ladders, had been drafted into the Auxiliary Fire Service and was on duty. Every time a bomb dropped she bent her head and stifled a sob with her handkerchief. My parents, Bill and me made the little cellar rather crowded. In addition, the yard's population was increased by the presence of George Rastrick, whose mother now kept the corner shop, and his fiancée Elsie, who had been visiting the Garlicks and had decided to stay when the sirens sounded. George was short, stocky, and balding, but a very natty dresser with a liking for Barney Goodman suits. He was also an authority on aeroplanes and had an impressive collection of them which he had painstakingly modelled from balsa wood. 'Them's Jerry planes!' he suddenly exclaimed during a slight lull in the bombardment, 'Listen.' We all listened fearfully to a strange, uneven throbbing, which sounded all too close. 'They make a noise like that because their engines aren't synchronised,' quoth the expert. 'They're not as good as ours.' This technical British superiority seemed of little consequence to me as I struggled to subdue a rising panic and stop my legs from trembling each time a bomb dropped.

About midnight, the raid intensified. A series of heavy explosions culminated in one so near it seemed to lift the house, causing showers of whitewash to fall from the ceiling. This annoyed Mrs Garlick so much that she rushed up to the cellar head for a dustpan and a brush, which she applied with immense vigour under everyone's raised feet.

At one time I thought that she was about to give us all a going over, for we each had a white coating on our heads and shoulders. A few times I heard a distant banging, which George claimed were our Ack-Ack guns, but this was soon drowned by bomb blasts. Once again, Jerry hadn't played fair. It seemed to me that they had found an easy way into Sheffield, totally ignoring the seven hills that Fred Clayton had so definitely stated were impenetrable.

Slowly, my second 'Vigil on the Night' dragged endlessly on. With strained, pale faces, made whiter still by the deposit from the ceiling, we stared blankly at each other, wincing with fear at every near miss, praying for the dawn. Mr Garlick daringly went up to the kitchen and procured a white enamel bucket, which he placed halfway up the cellar steps, for use as a relief station. George Rastrick, who always liked to be the centre of attraction, started singing 'There'll Always Be An England', which we all falteringly tried to join in, but a tremendous explosion cut it short, just as we had got to 'while there's a country lane', making me think that there couldn't be much left of Clarence Street, let alone country lanes.

Just when I had got to a stage when cold, tired and paralysed with fright, half hoping that a direct hit would put us all out of our misery, I jerked upright and cocked my head on one side to hear better. Could it be? Yes it was, the blessed, long-prayed-for sound of the all clear: the long-awaited, strident, but yet exhilarating noise of the long-drawn-out wail heralding our release, at least for the time being, from the clutches of terror. 'Thank God for that,' said Mrs Garlick, with great feeling, with which we, as overnight converts to the power of prayer, agreed whole-heartedly.

Being nearest to the door, I was first up the cellar steps and into the back yard. Although it was just turned four o'clock on a winter's morning, the light of nearby fires and moonlight provided enough illumination for me to see the scenes of destruction. A cast-iron inspection grate cover in front of the outside lavatories had been blown up into the air from a direct hit on the sewer, thereby showering its fragrant contents liberally all over the yard and nearby houses. Pieces of newspaper, which only at the beginning of the week I had carefully cut into small squares and pierced with a nail, were plastered profusely on the walls like sodden posters. A strong stench of effluent contrasted sharply to the appetising aroma of frying bacon. 'Ar bet that's comin' from Burgon's warehouse,' cried Mr Garlick, pointing to a lurid glow in Bridgfield Road. I stumbled over slates and broken glass to our back door, which was hanging on one hinge, and was about to go into the house when a plaintive 'cheep', followed by a feeble attempt to chirrup, attracted my attention.

The living room window had been sucked outwards by the blast, along with the brown paper strips, the blackout blind and the long lace curtains. Entangled in this, hanging upside down, was the cage containing Charlie, our canary. Carefully turning it the right way up, all I could see in the glow of fires was a tiny, soot-blackened bundle of feathers, which only yesterday were as bright yellow as a newly-minted sovereign. Dad, Mam and Bill went into the house while I untangled Charlie's cage from the wreckage. I carried it inside. Dad had lit a candle. The water, gas and electricity had been cut off, the windows had been blown out, half the roof was missing and most of the living room ceiling was on the table, but otherwise things weren't too bad.

I took Charlie's body out of his cage. He was so tiny; it was impossible that something so frail and delicate could survive the blast from a high-explosive bomb, never mind being sucked through a window. After all, didn't colliers take a canary with them down the coalmine, because the wee bird was so sensitive to the first traces of gas? Carefully I wiped the soot and dirt from his feathers with a damp floorcloth, thinking that at least I could give him a decent, clean burial, when suddenly, a little pulsing tremor trembled through his tiny frame and his bright beady eyes slowly opened, blinked once or twice, then

twinkled, sharp and clear. Dad knew what to do. He filled Charlie's pot with some water from a saucepan that Mam always kept on the hob, then put in it a couple of drops of whisky from the bottle out of the threepence ha'penny club that he had been saving for Christmas. Charlie took a sip, then a few more, hopped up on to the top perch, cleared his throat, filled his chest with air, and there, amidst all the debris, crackle of fires and the crump of a delayed-action bomb, he trilled his heart out with one defiant melody after another.

At five o'clock in the morning, there seemed little we could do until daylight. Although we were all dog-tired, sleep seemed out of the question. We cleared up the living room and kitchen as best we could. The upstairs windows, strangely enough, were undamaged, although piles of soot had cascaded down the bedroom chimneys into the fireplaces. At least we could have a fire, and one was soon burning in the grate, alleviating the gloom a little.

With all the fires raging round about, there was no point in worrying about the blackout blinds not being in place, but it was very draughty. A kettle full of water left over from the night before was soon boiled. We all had a cup of tea, then Dad said, 'We'll have to see where we can get some water. It'll take them ages to get the mains mended.' He and Bill took the only two buckets we possessed and I carried the kettle. Warily we stumbled down Clarence Street. Most of the houses were minus windows, but strangely Beresford's and Sweetmeat Joe's were intact. We had no idea where to go for water. One or two people with buckets were wandering aimlessly about, until a man carrying two saucepans full of water came through the Arcade and shouted, 'If y' want sum watter, thi's a tap in Beeley Street.' A long queue of people snaked down the entry and onto the pavement, waiting patiently to get water from a solitary little brass tap, which miraculously still worked and which, until the bowsers came round the streets, was our only source of supply. Dad said he wanted to go back down Cemetery Road to see if the Royal Oak had survived. It had, but Barclay's Bank lower down was minus its top floor. The Moor, our favourite promenade and street of pleasure in winter or summer, was ablaze from end to end. It was a vast cavern of flames, which swirled and eddied away, only to meet again overhead.

A few firemen stood beside their engine, powerless without water. All they could do was, like us, watch helplessly. A great eruption of fire and sparks shot high into the air, as buildings collapsed. We could feel the scorching heat, even though we were well back. Dad took off his glasses to see better, and squinting against the glare exclaimed, 'Poor old Kenny, it looks as though his pub's had it. I hope he's OK.'

Back at home with the water, I had some bread and dripping for breakfast and completed my toilet with a wipe on the face with a damp cloth. Then at half past seven, I set off to walk to work. To avoid The Moor I went along Porter Street. A shelter had suffered a direct hit and men were digging for survivors. A row of still forms, each wrapped in a blanket, lay on the ground, strangely peaceful, as if asleep. Union Street was a tangle of bricks and broken glass. The Empire had been bombed; across the road the Three Horseshoes pub was a gutted, smoking shell, and on the other corner Brook Shaw's car showroom was badly damaged. The old Tivoli, scene of many cowboy epics, seemed to have escaped unscathed. Cooper Brothers had been hit, but not badly, and our little workshop was still intact. The workforce spent the day clearing up. Fortunately, the firm's safe had survived, and we all got paid our wages. Mr Little, still immaculate, told us that we could have Saturday morning off — an act of generosity never known before in the firm's long history.

On Sunday morning, after fetching water and eating a cold breakfast, I set off with Dad for a walk up The Moor. A way had been cleared through the masses of rubble and the burnt-out shell of a tramcar moved to the side of the road. What had been fine shops, banks and pubs only

two days before were now smoking, gutted ruins, some with girder work bent and distorted as if in agony, others with glassless windows revealing their shattered interiors. The Anvil, Kenny MacLeod's pub and one of Dad's favourite hostelries, was a smoke-blackened roofless skeleton of stone, its fine beautifully-etched windows blasted into fragments. My father blew his nose loudly, his face tinged with sadness as his hand went up to his trilby, which he doffed in a silent tribute to the happy times that had gone forever.

Up The Moor came the slight figure of Mr Lem, the deaf engraver and a fellow son of suction of Dad's, daintily picking his way over the rubble like a cat on broken eggshells. 'Good morning, Sid' and a friendly nod to me was his greeting. To my father's reply of 'A terrible business this is, Tom,' he answered, 'Yes, it is a bit nippy this morning, Sid. I've just been down to look at my shop — it's alright!'

Dad took hold of Mr Lem's arm and cupping his hand, bellowed into his ear, 'How did you get on, Thursday night?' I knew that the engraver's custom every night upon finishing work in Bowden Street was to stroll down to Kenny's, then at quarter-past seven prompt come out and catch a tram to his home in Carrington Road. Mr Lem, nodding his understanding of the enquiry, answered, 'Well, Sid, I came out of the pub and saw my tram waiting across the road. I thought, it's a bit early, but still, I went upstairs, lit my pipe and started to read the Telegraph. I must have been there about five minutes and began to think it's funny we haven't started and there's only me on the top deck. All of a sudden, from behind, somebody shook my shoulder. It was a bobby in a tin hat, and he shouted, "Come on out of it, you silly owd sod — bloody tram's on fire!" When we got down on the ground, he pointed under the tram and by God, it was well alight!' He chuckled at this reminiscence, sucking contentedly at his pipe, and I wondered if deafness was such an affliction. At least he'd never heard the terrifying scream of a falling bomb, or the nerve-shattering crump of high explosive.

Bidding farewell to Mr Lem, we continued our sad shamble up The Moor. Atkinson's fine store and Marks and Spencer's, which were built only a year or so ago, were totally wrecked. The new building of Williams Deacons Bank at the corner of Rockingham Street gaped wide open to the public gaze, having had its front completely blown off. On that bitterly cold grey December morning, young though I was, memories of happy times on The Moor came flooding back to me, and I said to Dad, 'I don't want to go any further.' He nodded. For the first time in my life I saw tears in his eyes as, unlike him, he put an arm around my shoulders and we walked slowly home.

Chapter 15

Two New Jobs

*I*T BECAME EVIDENT, even at Cooper Brothers, that the war was getting serious. The Jerries invaded Greece and Yugoslavia, the production of the tea and sugar containers was terminated, and Mr Beardsall told me, 'Mr Little says that you and me have to work on the machines in the press shop.' My heart fell, but he continued, 'If you want, while you're still sixteen, you are free to get another job, but when you reach seventeen, you can be directed anywhere by the Government.' He also informed me that the College of Art had been so badly damaged that the silversmithing class had been discontinued for the foreseeable future. I still had the child's cup and bowl, but the unfinished plate that was to complete the set lay under tons of rubble.

It looked to me as though my ambition to be a second Benvenuto Cellini had been nipped in the bud. However, as I walked home I didn't feel too bad about this new phase of my career. At sixteen, with all the optimism of youth, the world was my oyster, just waiting to be opened. A verse, one of many that Edgar was so fond of quoting, came back to me, lifting my spirits. I recited it aloud:

> *It matters not how strait the gate,*
> *How charged with punishments the scroll,*
> *I am the master of my fate:*
> *I am the captain of my soul.*

A rag and bone man, resting at the side of his barrow in Clarence Street, heard me, shook his head and tapped his temple with a dirty forefinger and looked meaningfully up into the sky. When I told Dad about my situation, he chuckled, 'That's funny, I called into Arthur Rogerson's for a drink and Harry Benton, an old pal of mine, happened to mention that he was looking for a lad to work for him and learn die-sinking.'

Mam looked worried at this remark and queried, 'Won't the dye get on our Georgie's chest? You know how delicate he is.' On being reassured that this would not be the case, Dad said that he would contact Harry Benton and arrange for an interview with him. This he did, and a few days later, I walked up Clarence Street to the time house entrance of Viner's in Bath Street. I was greeted by a one-armed old soldier, now a timekeeper, who informed me that his name was Bert Denham, and was then escorted by him to the workshop of Harry Benton, master die-sinker. This imposing hive of industry was a narrow, partitioned-off corner of the press shop. One side was taken up by shelves full of dies and at the other, near the windows, a bench ran the full length of the shop. A foot-treadled grindstone in an iron trough of water was the only piece of machinery, and the heating was supplied by a small oil drum, punctured with holes and placed over a gas ring on the floor. After coming through the press shop and being frightened by the thudding steel monsters, the sight of this highly-sophisticated equipment cheered me up, and I felt that I could cope. My first impression, too, of Harry Benton was favourable. He was seated at the bench with a hammer in one hand and a chisel in the other, his entire body shaking in a paroxysm of silent coughing. The timekeeper grimaced in compassion and left me for my interview to begin.

Gradually the eruption faded away, the heaving shudders quietened down, then finally, with a tremendous cough, Harry cleared his throat into a piece of paper, which he chucked into the waste bin. 'That's better!' he gasped, wiping his eyes with a red-spotted handkerchief, then lighting a cigarette. Dad had said that my prospective gaffer's age was sixty-four, but viewed from the superiority of my callow sixteen years he looked like Methuselah. Heavily-built, and a little stooped, his face was deeply lined and bedecked with bushy grey eyebrows, from under which twinkled a pair of rheumy, blood-shot, but humorous brown eyes. What hair he had was short but thick, except for a large bald patch on top of his head, which seemed to have been plucked bare to supply tufts for his ears, nostrils and cheekbones. He wore heavy Derby tweed trousers and a waistcoat of the same material, liberally powdered with ash, because he never buttoned his brown smock. His footwear — black leather boots cobbled with tremendously thick soles and heels, — gave him an extra few inches in height, but, which he later confided in me, he had worn since he was a lad on account of having weak ankles and the extra weight might strengthen them.

I stood at the side of him whilst he outlined my duties. He said, 'You'll work for me. I'll pay you an' stamp y' cards, y'll not 'av t' clock in 'n y'll not need a pass to go out.' I thought this was great. Harry explained further. 'Viner's, when they had this factory built a few years ago, took in a lot o' the outworkers who used t' do work forrem, 'n let 'em have workshops rent free, 'n each gaffer pays his own lot 'n keeps what's left for hissen.' I was a bit disappointed when he told me that we worked on Saturday mornings, because Viner's was known for working a five-day week, the only firm doing so in the cutlery industry. Still, there was a war on. Later I was told the reason for turning in on Saturday was so that Harry, an inveterate backer of horses, could escape from his wife's surveillance to have a bet.

On my first morning I arrived early, opened up the shop, swept it out and lit the gas ring. Harry duly arrived, put down the old leather bowling bag in which he carried his dinner and the *Daily Herald*, took off his trilby and jacket and donned a soiled brown smock.

On his bench, chisels, punches and files of every description, from small rifflers to large bastards, lay in great profusion. 'Watch me for a bit, it'll give y' some idea,' he told me, lighting a cigarette. In front of him was an oblong tin box that had once contained 'Oxade' lemonade crystals. This was a resting place for Harry's cigarettes which, while I watched him work, burnt themselves out, leaving a little caterpillar of ash. At each blow of a hammer, this floated in the air like a miniature snowstorm, making Harry cough and sneeze. After a while, during which he had two fags on the go at the same time, one on the box and the other in his mouth, and I was beginning to wonder whether I had come to learn smoking as well as die-sinking, he took me to the end of the bench, where stood a huge round cast-iron die which was indented with the impression of a fire watcher's tin hat. This had to be scraped, riffled and stoned with carborundum sticks and finally polished to a very high standard with a mixture of oil and powdered emery.

For all my first morning as an apprentice die-sinker, I rubbed away, seemingly making very little progress, but Harry seemed satisfied when inbetween bouts of hammering and coughing he came over to me. Every few minutes the door opened and a workman walked in, had a word or two with Harry, a look at the back page of the *Daily Herald*, then left a slip of paper and some money on the bench. Just before dinner, Harry called me over to him. Handing me a bundle of papers and coins, he said, 'Come wi' me.' Off we went through the press shop. A lot of girls were working on machines and fly presses, and as I passed some of them whistled. At the time house, Bert Denham let us out on to the pavement. 'Nah then, George,' quoth Harry, pointing along Bath Street, 'See that chap in a raincoat, standin' at bottom of an entry?' I nodded. 'Right, just nip along an quick as y' can, gie 'im them slips 'n money an' don't let anybody see yer.' Off I went. As I approached my quarry, two men on opposite corners of Headford Street eyed me suspiciously, but seemingly satisfied they relaxed and resumed their loitering. I handed over my cargo, which was adroitly stuffed into the bulging pockets of the raincoat man. He was a man of medium build, sharp-featured with more colour in his cheeks than most people I knew. 'Thanks son. Ar ta Harry Benton's new lad?' was all that he said. It dawned on me that he was a street bookie, or at least stood for one, and he seemed quite a nice chap.

Every day, sometimes two or three times when there was a lot of meetings, I delivered betting slips and money. If there was anything to draw I went along to a little back-to-back house in Thomas Street, and, without knocking, entered into the abode of Mr Harrison. No matter

what the weather was like outside, a bright coal fire glowed in the grate of a black-leaded Yorkshire range. Ornaments, pictures and highly-polished heavy furniture blended with the mouthwatering aroma of freshly-baked bread cakes to create a peaceful little haven, especially in winter.

In the middle of the room stood a big scrubbed table without a cloth, but covered instead with betting slips, piles of coins and even bank-notes. Mrs Harrison, neat and tidy as her house, and always with her hair neatly coiffured, could reckon up the most complicated bet in a few seconds and knew to a penny how much to pay out. She was always smiling, even when paying out a large sum of money, and sometimes, when the amount was small, she handed me half a still-warm-from-the-oven bread cake, liberally spread with dripping. I enjoyed this treat, and looked forward to a day when there was little to draw, although Harry Benton and the rest of Viner's punters didn't.

Chapter 16

Training for Fire Fighting

*T*HE OLD PROVERB 'Locking the stable door after the horse has bolted' proved correct when, some time after the blitz, the Government issued an order that teams of fire watchers must be formed to protect houses and factories.

Accordingly, groups of men over the age of sixteen, including myself, were directed to St Silas, my old school, for courses of instruction on dealing with enemy conflagrations. During the last big air raid, the Luftwaffe had rained down on Sheffield hundreds of high-explosive bombs, several land mines and thousands of incendiary bombs. To save Sheffield from destruction if this were to happen again, each team was issued with a bucket to contain water, a stirrup pump, sand, a long-handled scoop and a dustbin lid.

On a pleasant summer evening in 1941, little groups of men and youths carrying this equipment straggled past the big wooden gate into my old playground. An officer from the AFS lined us up in some semblance of order and proceeded to tell us what to do in the event of an attack from the air.

Geo. Cunningham

'What you 'ave t' do when an incendiary bomb falls near is operate in teams of three. The leading man runs with the hosepipe as near as 'e can to the missile, flings 'imself flat on the ground, an' shouts in a loud, clear voice, "Water on!"' He paused, allowing time for this to sink in, before continuing. 'On hearing this, the man in charge of the stirrup pump will commence pumping. The jet of water will be directed by the hose-man, *not* on the bomb, but on the conflagration it has caused.' Again he stopped talking, looking enquiringly at us in case it was becoming too complicated. 'The man with the scoop, protected by the bin lid, can cover the bomb with sand, then convey it to a place where it can do no 'arm.' Our gallant team of fire fighters consisted of Georgie Hill on the hose, my father working the pump and yours truly with the bin lid and the scoop, because I had long arms.

The instructor ignited a smoke canister, to simulate an incendiary in a corner of the yard, bellowed 'Action stations!' and we sprang into activity. Georgie, a heavily-built forge hand, still wearing a sweat towel and clogs because he hadn't had time to change, lumbered across the yard with the hosepipe, uncoiling it as he went. He was going well, at a fair lick, when he stumbled, the pipe tangled around his legs and brought him down with a tremendous crash onto the asphalt. The pipe jerked the stirrup pump, causing the bucket of water to cascade over the yard and my father's shoes.

Georgie gallantly heaved himself upright and broke into a gallop, dragging behind him the hosepipe, stirrup pump and the empty iron bucket. He pitched headlong onto the ground as he neared the target, raised the nozzle triumphantly aloft and trumpeted, loud and clear, 'Watta on!'

I had my scoop full of sand ready to cover the bomb, but, when I tried to lift it, it was too heavy, and anyway the smoke was making me cough so badly I had to drop the scoop, and, with shield lowered, I leant against the wall like a stricken gladiator awaiting the *coup de grâce*. In the silence that followed this performance, my eyes cleared long enough for me to observe our instructor take off his cap, and for a moment I thought he was about to fling it to the ground and stamp on it in his chagrin. Instead, he closed his eyes for a few seconds, as if praying for guidance, scratched his head, replaced his cap and muttered quietly, but with feeling, 'F∗∗∗ me!'

Chapter 17

Fire Watching, a Fylfot and First Aid

SOON AFTER this episode, squads of fire watchers were formed at Viner's, consisting of eight men, of which I was one, probably due to me being experienced in dealing with conflagrations. The hours of duty were from seven o'clock at night until seven next morning. A command post was situated in a little-used cutlery warehouse on the second floor and was fully equipped for dealing with enemy action with a full-sized snooker table, eight bunks and a dart board. My squad, all of them older than me, was made up of: Bill Evans, who was a sixty-year-old cutlery forger; a spoon and fork stamper, Ernest 'Mac' Coles; Fred Naylor, the silver spinner; Harry Bagshaw, stamper; Squire Rodgers, collier; Alfie Farmer, spare lad; and Stan 'Curly' Watson, stamper.

Alfie, whom Mother Nature hadn't blessed with a full amount of grey matter, was nevertheless very useful for performing minor tasks in the forge. Early in the war, the clock in this department stopped, never to go again, and every so often Alfie was sent to the time house to see what the time was. Unfortunately, Alfie couldn't tell the time and when he enquired he was told any hour, just for a laugh. To combat this, Bill Evans told him to hold his arms in the same position as those on the clock face and keep them like that until he got back to the forge. The snag with this ingenious system was that, on the return journey, some joker would waylay Alfie and keep him talking for so long that his arm clock was always slow.

Stan Watson, thin to a state of emaciation, could still work long hours as a drop forger, existing on nothing more than tea and fags. He was in his late fifties, with false teeth so large they kept his lips from meeting, and high cheekbones, bossily prominent under the waxy, tightly-drawn skin.

We quickly developed a well-organised routine of snooker, darts and cards, and apart from a couple of false alarms the Luftwaffe, as if aware of our thorough training and strict discipline, left us alone. As a break from the severity of this nocturnal grind, a rota was drawn up allowing two at a time half an hour to visit any nearby hostelry. One night, Curly and Bill stayed out longer than usual and came back a bit kalied. Curly didn't bother taking off his boots, but slumped prone on his bunk and went out like a light. Nobody kept watch. We all retired, and in the dim blue glow of the night lamps the entire fire watching squad slumbered peacefully on.

I seemed to have been asleep for only a few minutes when I awoke, wondering where I was, until on the just-discernible clock I saw that there was still an hour to go before I need rise. Somehow, try though I might, further sleep eluded me, so I sat up, thinking that I might go for a walk before breakfast. My early morning yawn stopped in mid gape when at the top end of the bunk next to mine I could see a ghastly white skull with a black swastika desecrating it. Horror wiped away the last vestiges of sleep. I was transfixed. Had the Germans parachuted in a special unit during the night to massacre my comrades? Perhaps they had been disturbed before they got to me. Relief took over from these awful conjectures when I heard Mac snore and Squire Rodgers mumble in his sleep. I counted the rest of the motionless forms to make sure that none had been taken as hostages until I plucked up the courage to investigate the grisly remains. It was Curly, flat on his back, mouth open in a macabre toothful grimace with the hated symbol of the Third Reich painted on the top of his head. Who had visited him in the night I never found out, although when we all got up, Mac gave me a sideways nod of the head and a knowing wink. None of us said anything to Curly, who didn't bother with a wash, but just lit a fag and slouched off downstairs to the forge and started work.

Later that day, I was busy working on a die for a Bofor gun part when Squire came into the shop, laughing his head off. 'Owd Curly,' he gasped, inbetween chuckles, 'wor stampin' away on 'is 'ammer, when 'gaffer cum round wi' a party o' visitors. Thi wor sum big nobs from Government wantin' ter see wot we were dooin' fer waar effort.' Squire had to stop for another chortle before he carried on. 'Thi walked darn foorge, noddin' their 'eeads as if thi understood what wor gooin' off, when thi stopped in front o' Curly's 'ammer. He wor stood up, wire brushin' scale art o' top die, and when 'e'd dun that 'e bent o'er to do bottom un.' Squire had to pause again to wipe his eyes. 'Tha shud 'a seen the faces, when thi saw bloody swastika! Gaffer dashed round to Curly, but couldn't mek 'im understand becuss o' noise o' goffin 'ammers. Owd Curly kept purrin' 'is 'and on top o' 'is 'eead, but couldn't feel nowt, so 'e just carried on stampin'. One o' big nobs collared 'owd o' Alfie 'oo wor 'angin' abart 'n asked 'im 'oo bloke were an' wot 'ee were doin' wi a swastika on 'is 'eead.' Squire collapsed on my bench, and gasped. 'Owd Mac 'ad towd Alfie this mornin' that Curly 'ad been on 'oliday to Belsen and 'ad 'is 'eead tattooed as a souvenir, so Alfie sed same to this bloke! When ar cum art o' shop, thi wor orl mumblin' together 'n one on 'em wor writin' summat in his notebook.'

A few nights later I was on duty again, and just after ten o'clock, having made a personal best break of fifteen at snooker and thinking about retiring (to bed, not from a career in snooker), the command

post door burst open and in staggered the blood-stained figure of Harry Bagshaw. He was supported by Bill Evans, who himself looked as though he could do with some assistance. We gathered round the sorry pair and sat Baggy in a chair. 'Wot's up?' everybody said at the same time. Bill lit a Woodbine. 'Wi nipped across to 'Dog and Gun and Baggy, 'oo'd gorra bit o' bonus this week, started knockin' ale back as if waar wor o'er. 'E 'ad six pints in hafe 'n 'our 'n 'e wuda 'ad moor if ar 'anta dragged 'im art.' Pausing for a drag. 'Wi gorra cross rooad awreight, 'e wor wobblin a bit an' plattin' 'is legs when wi got back to 'firm.' He blew out a cloud of smoke and carried on. ''E wor doin' well 'til we were cumin' up them stooan steps. Near t' top Baggy missed one 'n slared darn rest on 'em on 'is chin.' Another drag before he continued. 'When ar gorra 'owd on 'im t' pick 'im up, 'e pulled hafe a bottle o' whisky art o' 'is pocket. It wor nearly empty. 'E said 'e'd gorra cowd cumin' on an' thowt 'e'd 'av a nip when 'e went t' gents in Gun.'

The wounded hero, seated in his chair beaming vacantly, looked as though he was enjoying his audience and our interest in his condition. Mac went to the sink and came back carrying a wet rag, with which he sponged some of the blood from Baggy's face, revealing a gaping gash running all along the chin bone. Bill Evans shouted, 'Tha looks as though tha's got two bleedin' gobs!' I went to the first aid cabinet, opened it and found the entire contents consisted of an empty iodine bottle, a black eyepatch and a finger stall, which looked as though it had been used. I came back to the casualty and showed the rest of the squad what our surgical resources were. We gazed helplessly at Baggy; the bit of rag was totally inadequate to staunch the flow of blood and it looked as though he'd had it. Suddenly Mac cried out, 'Ar know!' and dashed out of the room. In a couple of minutes he returned, holding triumphantly aloft in each hand a sanitary towel. 'Ar knew thi'd be sum o' these in wimmin's lav. Thi'll bi just the job!' So they were. They fitted snugly under Baggy's chin, the loops were tied with string onto the top of his head and the flow of blood was contained. Mac, pleased with his effort, stood back in admiration and exclaimed, 'Ar allus thowt tha wor a fanny merchant, Baggy, an' nar tha looks like one!'

It was evident, though, that in spite of this admirable emergency dressing, Harry's wound needed stitching, so after some deliberation Squire and myself were instructed to escort the casualty up to the Royal Hospital. Away from the warmth of the factory, the night was cold, wet and very dark. I was on the outside, Baggy in the middle, with Squire supporting him and guiding him away from the walls. Along Bath Street we lurched, up Thomas Street and along Broomhall Street. Not a soul was about. The Bath Hotel and the Albert were closed and shuttered. We bumped into something which Squire apologised to, before he found it was a pile of sandbags protecting an air raid shelter entrance, then finally we turned into Westfield Terrace.

The impressive portico of the old Mount Zion Chapel was the entrance to the hospital casualty department and I wondered what those worshippers of long ago would have thought about our motley trio as we stumbled up the steps between the huge stone pillars. We entered a large high-ceilinged, dimly-lit room, furnished with long rows of wooden benches. A marble mosaic floor and gloss-painted green walls did little to warm the flesh or cheer the soul in this sanctuary for the suffering. At the far end, a desk with a shaded lamp provided a welcome pool of light, which we made for. Behind the desk, stiffly starched in immaculate white, sat a nurse. Head down, she was busily writing in a large book. We lined up in front of the desk. She still wrote quickly onwards, a frown wrinkling her forehead, which increased as I coughed to make her aware of our presence. Closing the book, she put the cap on her fountain pen, screwed it tightly down and looked over the top of her spectacles. Dispassionately she surveyed our trio of gallant fire watchers. Squire and myself were both tall and skinny, wearing washed-out boiler suits which we had outgrown, so that the legs were inches shorter than the trousers underneath. Baggy, inbetween us, was short and fat, sporting a union flannel shirt and corduroys. Being toothless, and because the dressing was so tight, it had drawn up his bottom lip so that it almost touched his nose. It also had the effect of spreading his mouth into an idiotic grin that gave him the appearance of enjoying himself.

Dried blood on his shirt front, and an aroma of stale Gilmour's Windsor ale blended with whisky which he exuded as he swayed between us, hardly made him a rival to Ronald Colman. 'Name and address?' came the sharp enquiry. Baggy made a spirited attempt to reply, but could manage only a wide, imbecilic grimace and an unintelligible mumble, so, knowing where he lived, I answered for him. 'What's the nature of your injury?' was the next question. This time Squire spoke up on Baggy's behalf. ''E wor fire watching an' thowt 'e 'eard sirens an' wor rushin' up steps t' roof when 'e tripped an' cum darn 'em on 'is chin.' A disbelieving sniff from the nurse was followed by: 'Sit down and tell him to come when you hear the bell.' She departed down a dark passage behind her desk and we sat down on the cold hard highly-polished benches. The time dragged on. We seemed to have been there for ages; not even the tick of a clock broke the silence, and the only illumination was the light over the desk.

Baggy, who was propped between Squire and myself and had been so quiet that I thought he had fallen asleep, leaned heavily over to my side. I eased away to give him more room, trying to make things a little more comfortable for him. He inclined over to an even more acute angle, steadied himself, paused and then broke wind. In the stillness of the big room, amplified by the shiny wooden bench, bare walls and marble floor, it sounded like a coarse linen sheet being rent from top to bottom. The last echoes faded away. Baggy sat back on the bench with a relieved and contented expression on his face, his grin wider than ever. Out of the gloom behind the desk light, the white figure of the nurse quickly emerged. 'I heard a noise — is he in pain?' she snapped. 'Not anymore miss, he's got over it,' I replied. Squire, though, who had been the unfortunate recipient of the malodorous emission, mumbled through the handkerchief he held over his nose, 'Ar bloody well 'aven't.' A bell rang. Spurred on by a push from me, Baggy answered the summons and lurched off down the passage to emerge a few minutes later with a neat dressing around his chin.

On our way back to the firm, stumbling along in the bitter, black coldness of the night, Baggy became querulous, complaining that his new bandage 'Weren't as waarm as first un. That theer doctor said to me, "'Oo purrit on? 'E ort ter bi werkin' at Jessop 'ospital."' Swaddled, grey-blanketed forms, from which emanated an irregular chorus of snores, groans and the occasional sigh, assured me that the fire watchers were at their usual state of alert readiness when we arrived back at our command post. In the dim, blue light, I wrote in the incident book particulars of our first casualty. Squire mashed a mug of tea, from which we all sipped gratefully, although Baggy experienced a little discomfort because his wound was stiffening up. The tea refreshed him somewhat; he revived, and exclaimed cheerfully and loudly, 'Arve not 'ad a bad neet. Owt's betta dan bein' at 'ooam wi' towd lass.' A polite request from a disturbed comrade to 'Shurrup clackin', twat!' was acted upon, and the three of us joined the rest in a sweet repose.

Chapter 18
The Fighting 69th

*T*HE YEAR was 1942. I was seventeen and had been declared exempt from military service because I was in a reserved occupation. In any case, I don't think that I would have passed a medical. The days spent crouched over a bench and the long, fire-watching nights, of which I often did two a week for chaps who didn't want to spend a night away from home, had done little to improve my physical condition.

The war was at a crucial stage. The Jerries were still advancing in Russia, the Japs over-running the Far East. Singapore fell, and so did Tobruk, and I received a missive from the War Office calling me to serve my King and Country in the Home Guard. I duly reported, as ordered, and enrolled at Edmund Road drill hall, where I and several more soldiers of fortune were issued with khaki battledress, leather gaiters, a greatcoat, tin hat, military gas mask and a pair of ammunition boots, and told to attend parade next evening. This I did and we were shuffled into ranks by ex-regular army retired Sergeant Major Gibson. He was tall and stiff-backed, close-cropped and dapper, with two rows of ribbons on his chest. Up and down the straggly lines he slowly marched. As he passed in front of me, I thought I could detect in his eyes a slight look of disbelief that somehow he had to train us into a fighting machine capable of defeating the Wehrmacht if it invaded England. I was a teenager, over six feet tall; the man next to me looked to be about fifty and was about five feet four, and as nearly all of us were factory hands, pallid complexions and rounded shoulders were much in evidence.

We paraded three nights a week and Sunday mornings, and in a month or so we were marching up and down the wooden floor of the drill hall, stamping our feet like true guardsmen. Although we were shaping up like soldiers, there weren't enough rifles to go round, so the new recruits, such as me, had to make do with a pick shaft. We did have a World War One Vickers machine gun, but a notice had been hung over its barrel, stating 'This gun must *not* be used with live ammunition' — unnecessary really, because we hadn't got any.

On a cold autumn evening it was my turn to perform guard duty at the barrack gates. I stood there at the 'at ease' position, or at least my greatcoat did for, although the length was alright for me, it was wide enough for a man twice my weight, and the epaulettes, instead of being on the shoulders, were halfway down my arms. In an effort to make my chest appear bigger, I had stuffed, underneath my battledress blouse, the thick woollen scarf that Mam insisted on me wearing, but it wouldn't keep in place, persisting in slipping down to give me a pot belly. The pick shaft, which I had sandpapered and polished to a guardsman's standard, gave me some feeling of security, although I had little idea of its use, not having had any tuition in quarterstaff fighting, as had Errol Flynn in *The Adventures of Robin Hood*, which I had recently seen at the Star.

I was pondering on this theme and wondering what was for supper when the wicket gate behind me opened and out into the chilly night air stepped Sergeant Major Gibson. His eyes were rather red and an aroma of hops flavoured his breath as he enquired, 'Everything OK?' I snapped to attention and answered smartly, 'Yessir!' He looked up the deserted street, down the street and into the starry firmament and was about to go back to the warmth of the barrack room bar, when I plucked up courage and asked him, 'Sarnt major, if a German tank comes up Edmund Road, what shall I do?' His reply was immediate and delivered in a soldierly, convincing manner. 'Don't panic, keep outa sight 'til tank's a few yards away. Driver's only got a narrer slit to look through, so all yer've got ter do is run up an' jam yer pick shaft in it an' 'e'll not be able ter see weer 'e's goin!' This method of attack seemed to me to be a trifle chancy, so I pursued the matter further. 'What happens after I've done that?' Gibson looked at me, a little condescendingly, I thought, at my lack of initiative. 'Look,' he said, 'One o' crew'll oppen lid on top o' turret ter 'av a shufti.' I nodded my understanding. 'Right den,' spoke the gallant sergeant, 'Tek yer tin 'at off, unclip chin strap at one side, gerrowd o' end and whizz 'elmet round a coupla times, then let fly. It'll knock 'is bloody 'eead off!' I must have appeared still unconvinced at this unusual method of waging war, because Gibson carried on, 'David knocked art bleedin' Goliath same rooad dint 'e, an' *'e* wor bigger dan enny soddin' Jerry.' With that, he gave me a knowing nod, an encouraging pat on the back, then went through the gate, leaving me to mull over my first lesson in military tactics.

The next big event in my soldier's career happened when a consignment of 1917 Canadian Ross rifles arrived at the barracks. They were well greased, in excellent condition and sufficient in numbers to equip a platoon. The snag was that only a small amount of ammunition came with them, which had to be kept in reserve in case of an emergency, such as target practice for the officers, or an invasion.

We also had instruction on the Sten, a light machine gun that looked as though it had been made from bicycle parts. At least we were beginning to look like soldiers when we paraded. One pleasant spring evening, Gibson appeared in a good mood and addressed our ranks thus: 'We're gonna march up ter Norfolk Park an' ar'll teach yer summat about grenade throwin'.' This sounded a lot more exciting than barrack life and I could feel a sense of adventure well up inside of me as we marched through the gates and swung along Queens Road and turned up Granville Road. Our new arm badges drew an admiring shout from one of a group of lads hanging around the park gates. 'Look, the Fighting

Sixty-Ninth!' he yelled. Only last week I had been thrilled by a picture of that name, starring James Cagney, who saved his comrades by flinging his body over a German hand grenade before it exploded. It filled my heart with pride and patriotic zeal that I was a member of such a gallant troop, and prayed that something similar might happen which would enable me to prove my valour in the field. Up the path we marched. A child in a pram gazed at us in amazement then burst into tears, enraging its mother, but a salute from a chap with one leg and a crutch encouraged us on.

Led by the intrepid Sergeant Major Gibson, that hardened veteran of many Great War battles, I — and I am sure all the others as well — felt capable of tackling anything that could be brought up against us. On my right marched Brian Wildgoose, a big powerfully-built thirty-year-old from Loxley, nicknamed 'Big Okker' because he was a ganister miner and always came home from work plentifully plastered with ochre, a kind of yellowish clay. I had seen him play cricket. He was a fair batsman, but his bowling and throwing-in were a little erratic, to say the least, because he had only one eye and the other was usually half closed by a chronic stye.

We halted at the foot of a grassy slope at the top of which was a small cafe, about a hundred yards from us. 'Right men,' Gibson whispered quietly, so that the enemy couldn't hear. 'Six o' you run, bent darn, wi' two bombs apiece. Rest on us'll bi behind, firin' ter cover yer.' He continued, 'Enemy trench's is dat deer stooan wall, twenny yards ter left o' cafe.' He motioned the bomb carrier, Dicky Andrews from Moore Street, to come forward. Out of a canvas sack were produced the deadly missiles. I had the honour to be in the first wave alongside Okker, and I waited impatiently whilst Gibson instructed, 'Dees ar dummies, dis no explosive in 'em, but thi same weight as real uns.' He lined the six of us up behind the cover of some nearby bushes. 'OK den, all y've got ter do is run like hell, den when y'r in range, pull 'pin art, count five, throw grenade, lay flat forrabit, den chuck next un.' This was more like the real thing, I thought, feeling for the first time the satisfying weight of a Mills bomb.

On the word of command we set off, pounding up the slope to our objective. Battle fury surged through me, the exhilaration engendered by the charge lent wings to my heels. I curbed my impatience, trying to get as close to the enemy as I could. I thought that we were still well out of range, with about fifty yards to go, when Big Okker bellowed out a cry of defiance: 'Tek dat, y' lousy bleeders!', arched his arm back, and with all his considerable strength let fly the first grenade. I threw myself flat and from under the rim of my tin hat watched the flight of the missile. At first I couldn't see it, because not only was it travelling very quickly, it was also well off target. Instead of landing in the enemy trench, the grenade went clean through the cafe window. For a few seconds, after the crash of glass, there was silence, and forgetting all about the enemy I stood up, along with the rest of the squad, gaping at the damage. The window was a large one, and so was the hole in it. A woman's face appeared in the aperture, surveyed us with an expression of astonishment, which deepened into anger, then vanished. Gibson came up at the double. 'Wot the bloody 'ell were y' aimin' at?' he shouted, pulling Okker round to face him. 'Sorry Sarge,' mumbled the crestfallen giant, 'Ar gorrer a bit carried away, like.' It seemed that our spirited attack on the enemy front line had fizzled out. The rest of the platoon straggled up the slope to see what was going on. I stood, confused, with a bomb in each hand, waiting for the next order, as Sergeant Major Gibson marched purposefully up to the cafe. He had got within a few yards of his objective when the door opened and the lady whose face I had seen through the hole in the window came out.

She was well endowed. Mother Nature had been generous with her in every respect, blessing her with an ample bosom, wide hips and arms like hams. Her dress was informal: a flowery overall covered her

body but revealed the curves. Carpet slippers on her feet, hair in curlers and a florid complexion, puce-like with pent-up emotion, made a vision to behold on a pleasant spring evening in the park. In one beefy paw she clutched, Britannia-like, a large sweeping brush. The gallant sergeant, with ribbons on his chest to prove that he was not lacking in courage, scaled the grassy slope and spoke up. 'Arm sorry, missis, one o' my men . . .' was as far as he got before the agitated floodgates of the fair lady burst. 'Ar'll give thi sorry. Ar spent 'ours cleanin' bloody place up, an ar wor just gunna mek missen a nice cup o' tea, when sumbdy chucked a bleedin' bomb through winder!' Gibson held up both hands placatingly, 'Nar nar, luv, it wor an accident,' he wheedled, in a feeble attempt to calm the disgruntled matriarch. This approach only irritated Britannia even more and the sergeant major, rashly making the mistake of closing in on her, received from the sweeping brush a mighty thrust in the chest, which sent him staggering down the incline to end up ignominiously on his backside. He scrambled to his feet and tried again to carry on his conciliatory advances, when he saw that Britannia was following up the devastating lunge by mounting a full-scale charge. Although she had the strength, determination and armament to carry this out, her initial impetus was, by virtue of her considerable weight, a trifle sluggish. We weren't. With one accord we ran down the hill, routed and disorganised. Gibson at the rear, to try and save face, marched to cover our retreat at a quick, light infantry pace. The dulcet tones of our vanquisher shrieked after us. 'It's no good y' runnin', ar know weer y' from. Ar'll bi darn at them bloody barracks, just see if arm not!'

Behind the security of the shrubbery, I looked apprehensively back to see her brandishing the brush in a warning of further retribution. Gibson, although visibly shaken, now that the immediate danger was over regained his composure and instilled some discipline into his disorganised troops. 'Steady, lads. Get formed up, an' we'll 'av sum marchin'

drill.' This was greeted by a groan from the ranks, and Sidney, a fat little baker from Crookes who suffered from corns, muttered, 'We'd du better to learn some unarmed combat. Gibby might a' stood a chance wi' that woman den.'

We marched back down the same path that we had so confidently trod just a little while ago, but the spring was missing from our step, and shoulders that had been well squared were now bent. A final humiliation came as we passed through the park gates into Granville Road. The same group of lads were still gathered there and I brightened up a little, hoping that they, at least, would give us some encouragement. It was as if they could sense defeat, or perhaps just wanted something to do. What they did bestow on us was a sullen silence and a well-aimed apple core that whizzed from nowhere and ricocheted off my tin hat.

It was such a fine evening that Gibson, probably in an attempt to restore morale, marched us round the district for an hour or so, until finally, just as we were about to turn into Edmund Road, he abruptly halted the platoon. With a warning arm held out he whispered over his shoulder, 'Keep quiet, look 'oo's cumin art o' barracks.' In the twilight, dim, but plainly visible in the gateway, was the imposing figure of our conqueror. She was escorted by Lieutenant Finch, our platoon commander, whose weedy frame contrasted so much with Britannia's massive hulk that he looked to me like a tug alongside an ocean liner. As she sailed majestically away, the gallant officer saluted briskly and gave a little bow, which came more naturally to him because he was a shop floor walker at Walsh's. Gibson waited until the fair lady was well on her way, probably to the Royal Standard, before we marched into the barracks.

Immediately on our arrival, Finch hopped out of his office and piped, in his thin reedy falsetto, 'Sarnt Major Gibson, stand the men to attention!' We shuffled into ranks, stiffly upright, and awaited our fate. The lieutenant, highly conscious of his lofty rank, paced up and down before the first line, tapping a swagger stick against his leg and occasionally darting a watchful glance at us through steel-rimmed spectacles, before he finally said, impressively, 'I had a lady here tonight.' Okker muttered to me out of the side of his mouth 'Ar wish ar bleedin' 'ad.' Finch, pausing to lend full weight to his next words, continued, 'She made a very serious complaint about the conduct of this platoon, which resulted in serious damage to the cafe where she was engaged in cleaning.' He carried on, 'I think that it was only due to the tactful manner in which I handled this delicate situation that I have managed to settle the matter out of court.' A glint from the glasses in appreciation of the sigh of relief from his bored troops, which quickly turned into dismay as he trilled triumphantly, 'I have paid the good lady ten shillings to have the window repaired and for returning the hand grenade, and also an extra half-crown as compensation for the distress it has caused her. To cover this sum of money, I want sixpence from each man. Sarnt Gibson, dismiss the men and collect the money from them in the canteen.' He did a smart about-turn and skipped back into his office, slamming the door behind him as a signal that he would brook no argument. We trailed upstairs to the canteen, mumbling dismally about the cost of our outing, which amounted to the price of a pint per man.

Big Okker, like a true Englishman, rose to the occasion. Not noted for rhetoric, he simply said, 'It wor ma fault, ar'll stand 'joss.' A few barely-audible cries of 'Nay, nay,' and 'Tha waint, owd lad,' turned into laughter when the grenadier quelled the dissension by shouting, 'It wor worth ivvery penny just t' 'av seen dat owd lass purrowd Gibby on 'is arse!'

Chapter 19

In Town Tonight

*I*N SPITE OF the company of my workmates and the comradeship of the Home Guard, my social life was pretty dull. Bill was called up to serve in the Lincolnshire Regiment, Norman Blackwell worked all hours, and I had heard that Vinny had joined the RAF and was training as an air gunner. On the few free nights I had, it was my usual practice to drift into town. Barker's Pool was always a lively place: a speakers' platform at the corner of Holly Lane was a wooden beer crate borrowed from the Albert Hotel by a gentleman called Alf Marples, who claimed to represent the Independent Labour Party. A little stockily-built man with a loud voice, clad, like his hero Keir Hardie, in cloth cap and workaday clothes, he was quite a sight to behold when in full cry and riding his pet hobby horse — the repression and exploitation of the working class by the bloated plutocrats. As he ranted on, his voice became ever more hoarse, a film of spittle coated his lips, giving extra emphasis to his delivery, and also spraying the front rank of the faithful when he spat out some particularly caustic invecture.

'Believe me, brothers,' he bellowed, 'While you an' your wife an' children are shivering in front o' an empty grate, existin' on short rations, an' workin' all 'ours for a mere pittance, there are people up theer,' pointing an accusing finger in a westerly direction which traversed an arc that took in Millhouses, Nether Edge, Ecclesall and Fulwood, 'who are livin' on the fat o' the land. Them and their kids go short o' nothing!' There was a murmur of agreement, a ripple of applause and the odd 'Hear, hear!' from his supporters as I walked away, wondering how Mr Marples could know so much about the living conditions of the upper class. The steps of the City Hall, which, like its pillars, still bore the shrapnel marks from a bomb dropped during the blitz into the big static water tank in front of the War Memorial, were beginning to be lined by groups of young women — or at least quite a few of them had, at a distance, an appearance of youth. A fortunate few wore nylon stockings, but most of them had to make do with staining their legs, sometimes with gravy browning, then getting a friend with a steady hand to paint on the seams. For all that, they made a pretty picture, considering that many of them worked long hours at hard, dirty jobs and lived in back-to-back houses without a bathroom or inside lavatory.

A little group of them, primped and powdered up, were whiling away the time by putting pennies into the slot of a large telescope that was focused upon the figure of Vulcan on top of the Town Hall. It had been someone's bright idea that, to raise money for the war effort, a penny fee would be charged so that people could see where flying shrapnel had taken off one of his kneecaps. The girls, however, had other ideas. Vulcan, God of fire and metalworking, was twice as large as life and had everything in proportion, including his manhood, so, with him being in a state of nature, this attribute brought on fits of giggling from his girlish admirers. One of them, after being shoved out of the way by an eager friend, shrieked ecstatically, 'Bloody 'ell, it's gorra end on it like a blind cobbler's thumb!' — a remark that made the rest of her companions all the more impatient to have a peep. More and more 'girls' arrived, so that there was little room on the already-crowded steps.

The Town Hall clock and wristwatches were continually scrutinised. Last-minute pats of powder, touches of lipstick, quick glances in mirrors for assurance — even the telescope was abandoned when in the distance a sound of heavy motors could be heard, quietening the excitable chatter.

This was quickly kindled into an expectant cheer as up Fargate rolled a long convoy of big American Chevrolet trucks. The canvas tops were down, revealing their cargo of dough-boys. Up Barker's Pool they came like an invading army, turned round the Memorial and pulled up in front of the City Hall. Down from their perches like a colourful flock of prattling budgerigars the girls flew down to greet them, and in a matter of minutes all of them, even the old and ugly ones, were paired off. The GIs, some of them black, were immaculately clad in well-tailored khaki tunics, highly-polished brown shoes and peaked caps. Quite a few had rows of medal ribbons. Contrasting the smartness of this turn-out against my baggy, ill-fitting Home Guard battledress, gaiters and clumsy black ammunition boots, I realised that I would have no chance in competing for the favours of the opposite sex if I had arrived at Barker's Pool on a Sunday evening in my military accoutrements. The troops and their partners, making the most of the short time they would have together, were

90

quickly on their way to the pubs and dancehalls, and soon the square was almost empty except for a few strollers, the odd tab-end collector and a tiny knot of the die-hard proletariat still being harangued by Alf.

After the excitement caused by the American invasion, a feeling of loneliness crept over me, so in search of company — any sort would be preferable to my own — I walked across to the Albert Hotel at the top of Cambridge Street, but it was already packed to the doors. The easiest way was downhill, but the Sportsman too had a queue outside. In front of me Russian Edna, with a tightly-coiffured hairdo, fur collar and high heels, was clicking purposefully on her way to the Barley Corn, now nicknamed 'The American Embassy' because of its popularity with our erstwhile colonial cousins.

I hesitated outside the doors of this establishment, having heard from a chap at work of its reputation as a favourite haunt of the ladies of the night. The need for companionship over-ruled my principles, so in I went. Although it was early evening, the place was already crowded. On a stage at the top end of a large smoke-filled room, a big doughboy, capless and tieless, was giving a spirited performance on a set of drums, whilst the hapless civilian drum owner looked on apprehensively, wincing every time a tremendous crescendo threatened to split his precious drum skin. A saxophone player and a trumpeter made up the trio, both of them trying to outdo the other in a volume of sound as they rendered their own version of 'American Patrol'. I shouted above this racket, and through the blue haze of Camel and Chesterfield cigarette smoke, for a pint of bitter, and found a place at the corner of the bar. Everyone but me seemed to be having a good time. Some of the Yanks even had two girls, which wasn't difficult as they were dishing out largesse in the form of nylon stockings, bars of chocolate and packets of chewing gum. A girl, about my age, dark-haired and rather pretty, pushed her way through the crowd, and for a split second our eyes met. I felt my heart give a bound — could this be my lucky night? A

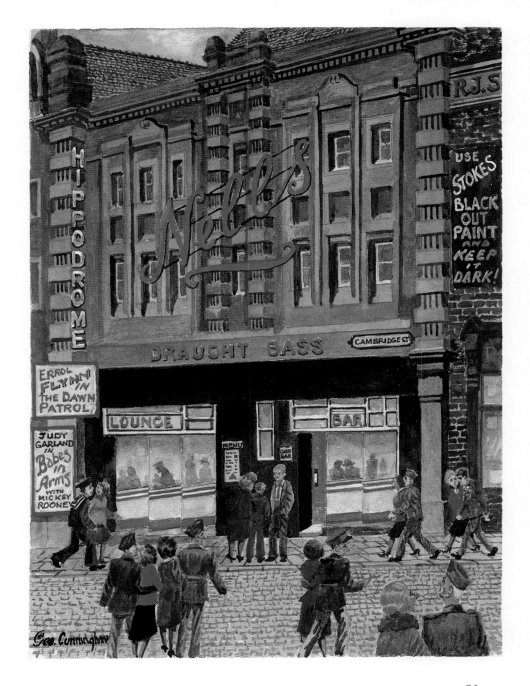

lightning top-to-toe summing up of me quickly wiped out whatever friendly feelings she may have had, even before a tall Clark Gable look-alike put his arm around her slender waist and drawled, 'What kinda drink will ya take, honey?'

Near the door, Russian Edna stood aloof. With the blessing of dim lighting and miasma of tobacco smoke, she appeared quite attractive in spite of advancing years. A burly sergeant, no chicken himself, went over to her and after a short conversation, which didn't alter the impassiveness of her features, they departed into the night. Finishing my pint, I emerged into Cambridge Street and wandered aimlessly down towards Nell's Bar. I thought it was a bit too posh for me, so I decided to push on to the Nelson at the Moorhead, where at least I could listen to the organ.

The posters outside the Hippodrome caught my eye: *The Dawn Patrol* starring Errol Flynn was on. I thought, what a pity the pictures don't open on Sundays, I would have lashed out ninepence for a seat in the gods. A familiar voice broke into my reverie: 'Nar den, Georgie, wot da doin' round 'ere, da'll get picked up if dar not careful!' It was Moxay, barely recognisable in a smart utility blue serge suit, with his hair plastered flat with Brylcreem. Clinging to his arm and gazing adoringly down at him was a lady old enough to be his mother. Taller than her escort, with her abundant charms both emphasised and constrained by the art of the corsetier, she was so heavily perfumed one could almost see a vapour of 'Evening in Paris' enveloping her. Thick lips, lavishly lacquered, and eyebrows plucked and pencilled into half-circles gave her podgy face an expression of permanent, inane surprise. She emitted a girlish giggle, coquettishly revealing lipstick-stained teeth, as Moxay introduced her. 'Dis is Lily. She's gorra corner shop in Darnall, an' arm lookin' after 'er, cus 'er 'usband's in Navy, an' she gets a bit lonely at times, don't y' luv?' I almost envied him; at least he had some company. Moxay appeared quite affluent, producing a chromium cigarette case filled with Turf, expertly ignited a match with his thumbnail and exhaled luxuriously, evidently well pleased with life. I asked him where he worked and he replied, 'At a little cutlery firm in Carver Street. Arm doin' a bit o' grindin'.' He must have noticed the slight grimace of contempt on my face, because he retorted, 'Don't dee look darn di nooas, Georgie, ar du fire watchin' four neets a week on t' factory.' I still was puzzled why this could be lucrative enough to provide him with his evidently expensive lifestyle until he continued, 'Da knows town's full o' Yanks every neet? Well, ar let mi bunk off fer five bob an hour, so dat di can cum sumweer quiet wi' a lady friend, an' discuss waar situation. While di gerrin' on wi' it, arm in next room wi' mi feet up.'

We were about to part. Lily, obviously disinterested in me, was steering Moxay into Nell's, when suddenly down the street came a vision in green. At least that was the effect it had on me. A crown of flame-coloured hair adorning a charming freckled face, contrasting vividly with the colour of her coat, long slim legs and red high-heeled shoes, blended to create an impression powerful enough to make my bottom jaw drop. Who is she? Where have I seen her before? Moxay shattered my romantic trance and brought me back into the world of reality by addressing the goddess in an engaging manner. 'Ey oop lass, weer da guin', darn eer on di own? Ant ta 'ad enny luck terneet?' The deity didn't waste words on him, dismissing his vulgar query with a contemptuous glance and a toss of her carmine crown. A spark of recognition blazed into flame, when I suddenly realised that this earthbound angel was none other than Moxay's sister, Molly. What miracle had transformed a gap-toothed skinny wisp of a child into a beautiful, self-assured woman was beyond me, as I stood there, transfixed and tongue-tied. Her brother had no such inhibitions. 'Da knows 'oo 'e is, lass, 'e's pickle man's lad, Georgie Cunningham, aren't ta?' Assuming an air of a man-about-town nonchalance, copied from Cary Grant, I gulped, 'Yes,'

and stood there red-faced and stuck for words. Lily, unwilling to share him with anyone, tugged her paramour into Nell's, leaving his sister and me outside.

Evidently they felt no need for our company, but I wished that they had stayed with us longer. 'Fancy a drink?' was my next conversational gem. 'No,' she replied, barely moving those ruby lips and shimmered off down the street. I walked beside her. She appeared not to resent my presence, although she wasn't exactly talkative. In fact, after that monosyllable, she never uttered a word. We turned onto Button Lane. I was tempted to ask again if she would partake of a drink in the Angel, but feared a refusal. Occasionally we brushed against each other, but she made no attempt to link my arm and I respected her maidenly innocence by keeping my hands to myself. All too soon we arrived at Headford Street. Time was running short, so plucking up courage I halted a few yards from the Moxay residence and blurted, 'What about goin' t' Star wi me next Satday?' Perhaps a shade too quickly she, without seeming to part her lips, murmured, 'See y' outside, seven o'clock,' and smartly tapped away on her red high heels. In the gathering dusk I watched until she got to her door, where she stopped, then very slowly turned around and lifted her hand. Was it my fancy, or a trick of the twilight, a casual farewell gesture, or did she actually blow me a kiss? Whatever she did, it transformed dingy, blacked-out Moore Street's pavements into a magic carpet, which carried me home without my feet touching the ground.

Chapter 20

A Fine Romance

THE FOLLOWING WEEK seemed to stretch into a year, lengthened by the long hours of fire watching and Home Guard duties. I had only one free evening and I spent an hour in the blackout, lurking at the corner of Molly's street, hoping to catch a glimpse of her. Once the door did open, my heart leaped, but it was only Mrs Moxay chucking out the cat, which miaowed resentfully before arching its back and elevating its tail to spray the doorstep with its own lingering brand of perfume. At long last Friday came. Harry Benton paid me my wages and my plan began to take shape. I bought some sweet ration coupons from Taff in the press shop, which I could add to mine, making enough to buy a pound box of milk chocolates. On Saturday evening I took extra care over my toilet, straightening my tie and brushing an unruly lock of hair into submission. I could see, in the mirror, Mam watching me.

I said casually, 'I might be a bit late home. I'm going to the second house at the Star.' She gave a knowing look, but didn't say anything in reply beyond 'Be careful!' A caution such as that was the last thing with which to admonish the young Lochinvar, preparatory to his first long-awaited romantic rendezvous. Up Ecclesall Road I blithely stepped, admiring my reflection in Osbert Skinner's window and went into Alex Korklin's spice shop, plonked down half a crown and the coupons, and asked for a pound of Dairy Box. The confectioner's face lit up at the sight of such a big spender and he quickly produced from under the counter a box of the delectables. Outside the Star a small queue

had begun to form under the canopy. I was early. I had checked the time with Skinner's clock. A couple of overcoated, under-age lads approached me. 'Tek us in mester,' the elder one pleaded, offering the admission money. It wasn't all that long ago since Bill and myself were doing the same as these lads, asking an adult to take us in to see an 'A' film, but I replied, exalted by my mature status, 'Sorry, son, I'm waitin' for sumdy.' The minutes slowly dragged on, a clock inside the foyer showed that she was five minutes late, but I consoled myself with the fact that it was half an hour to the start of the second house and there weren't many people in the queue. Molly came to me as unexpectedly as she had done in town, her Titian hair shining like a halo amongst the nondescripts shuffling along Ecclesall Road. I went to meet her, so eager and yet trying not to hurry.

In my raincoat pocket the box of chocolates bumped reassuringly, giving me more confidence. 'Hello,' I said, clearing a throat that had suddenly gone dry. She smiled without opening her lips. Gallon's grocer's shop spun round, and with a sudden burst of audacity I croaked, 'What about going for a drink?' A slight declination of her head signified agreement and I actually had the temerity to lightly clasp her arm, as I escorted her up William Street to the Sunnyside Hotel. Once inside the lounge, I felt more in command of the situation, as I ordered a pint of bitter for myself and asked Molly what she would like to drink. Perhaps a baby Guinness? Bill Hoole, the landlord, shook his head gloomily, and answered 'All I got in that line is milk stout.' Molly didn't reply,

but nodded acquiescence. We sat, side by side, on the horse-hair land settle, her hands crossed demurely over the top of her handbag, which rested on her lap. Her skirt, stretched tightly over shapely thighs, was enhanced by the provocative pimple of a suspender fastener, indicating that she was wearing stockings, not leg paint.

She opened her bag, took out a paper packet of five Woodbines, lit one, then put the rest back, without offering them to me, for which I wasn't sorry, as my few attempts at smoking had always made me cough and feel dizzy. Although Molly didn't appear to drink quickly, her glass was soon empty and she didn't object when I had it filled once

more. My next romantic query was, 'Where d' you work?' Again that flicker of an enigmatic, closed-lipped simper, as she softly murmured, 'Needham, Veall an' Tyzack's on Milton Street.' Mundane words, but to me, with passion inflamed by her presence and the pint of Tennant's, they sounded heavenly.

There were still a few minutes to go. I didn't want another drink, but Molly did. In for a penny, in for a pound, I reflected, taking great care to pour the stout with a nice, creamy head on it. My angel drained her goblet down to the last regretful droplet, dabbed those Cupid-bow lips with a tiny, lace hankie, had a last, quick appraising scrutiny of her appearance in the mirror behind the bar, then together we crossed the cobbled street and entered Paradise.

There was plenty of time: an usherette was still spraying perfumed disinfectant to dispel the odour left by the first house patrons and the reek of tobacco smoke. In a moment of reckless abandon, I shelled out three shillings for two seats on the back row of the balcony. We got right in the middle so that we didn't have to stand for anyone wanting to pass. Just before the lights dimmed and the projectionist's beam tried to focus on the screen, I casually produced the Dairy Box, as if I were used to doing it every day, and presented them to Molly. I was elated by the sight of her surprised eyes and look of eager anticipation, as she quickly opened the box and popped a coffee cream into her mouth, then the look of sheer bliss as she tenderly swallowed the delicacy. I wasn't very much aware as to what was taking place on the screen — a Charlie Chase film and the newsreel of world-shattering war scenes, faded into insignificance by comparison with Molly. It rather surprised me, but caused no offence, that she didn't offer a chocolate, but I was a little taken aback when the lights came on for the interval to see that she had scoffed the first two layers. The ice cream lady made an appearance. I passed a shilling along the row and two large tubs of Wall's were handed back to us. Molly opened hers, expertly folded the cardboard cap in two and used it as a scoop. I was about halfway down my ice cream when she dropped the empty carton on the floor and started looking longingly at mine. Due to rationing, it wasn't possible to buy another, so I regretfully handed it to her. This was quickly disposed of and she returned to the chocolates.

The big picture, starring Shirley Temple in *Curly Top*, wasn't much cop, and tentatively I reached for Molly's hand. It was so small and soft in my work-hardened paw. I could feel the exciting warmth of a silk-clad leg against mine as I pressed closer. She didn't turn her head. In the dim light I marvelled at the beauty of those finely-chiselled features, eyes half-closed in ecstasy as her tantalising lips slowly moved. I wondered if I dare kiss them, when suddenly they parted slightly, as if in anticipation, then from them issued, slowly and quite small at first, but gradually expanding, a pink balloon of bubble gum. Fascinated, I watched it grow bigger and bigger, until finally, with a tiny 'pop' it burst. 'God Save the King' brought everyone to their feet, and as I stood to attention Molly finished the last chocolate, elegantly bent down, placed the empty box on the floor and gently side-footed it, along with the ice cream cartons, underneath the seat in front of her.

My heart pounded with delicious anticipation as we filed out with the crowd into moonlit Ecclesall Road. Little could they imagine, I thought, of the amorous raptures that Molly and her audacious lover would soon be enjoying. It wasn't far along Moore Street to where Molly lived, but I was relieved to see, especially as it was full moon, the ambulances being driven back into their depot, signalling the end of a purple alert. Molly walked rather slowly and once or twice I thought I heard a tiny, girlish hiccup, quickly surpressed. To comfort her, and also as a prelude to the pleasures of things to come, I gently squeezed that tiny hand again, a gesture returned with only slight enthusiasm, which I put down to her maidenly modesty. The time had now come to the point where, as Gilbert wrote all those years ago, 'Faint heart never won fair lady! Nothing venture, nothing win . . .'. So just before we reached Headford Street, I gently put my arm around her slender waist and guided her into an entry. In a second my other arm had clasped her tender, yielding body to mine. The moonlight bathed her face in a pearly glow as she raised it to me, with eyes meekly closed, the long lashes fluttering gently like a butterfly's wings. I was about to sip the ruby wine of her lips, encouraged by a tremor which passed through her frame. Just as I responded, another even greater surge followed, and she broke away from me. My first reaction, frustrated though I was, was that she had realised that she was about to be overcome with passion and could no longer trust herself with such an ardent love.

Her heels stopped clicking after a few steps, and I gave her a minute to compose herself. Just as I was about to join her, I heard a retching sound, and looking out of our love nest I saw by the light of the moon Molly, bent over at the edge of the causey, being sick into the gutter. Compassionately, I went to render

assistance. When I attempted to put an arm around her she petulantly knocked it aside. After a final agonised puke, she straightened up, wiped her eyes, gasped for breath and panted, 'It wor them bleedin' chocolates, thi couldn'a been fresh!' Considering that most of them laid unchewed in the gutter, I thought it a bit ungrateful of her to utter in such a critical manner the only words she had spoken all evening. Then, as she opened her mouth wide for yet another vomit, I saw the reason for her Mona Lisa look. Molly, my heart's desire, was toothless.

This time, when I left her at the corner of the street where she lived, she didn't turn around. There was no farewell wave or a blown kiss, only the heartbreaking sound of the door being slammed on my blighted hopes. I trudged, leaden-footed, back along a dark and dismal Moore Street, which only a few minutes earlier had been strewn with rose petals. Clouds had blanketed the moon and a steady drizzle was falling, and I began to understand why inconsolable men often joined the Foreign Legion to try and forget their unrequited love.

Chapter 21
A Night Out

THE ROAD to recovery seemed long and hard. One evening I strolled aimlessly up The Moor, not knowing, or really caring very much, what destiny would have in store for me. Most of the left hand of the once proud street's buildings, devastated by the blitz, had been cleared, the older ones' cellars filled in, and the rubble scraped level. Dad's haven of refuge, Kenny McLeod's pub, the scene of so many convivial evenings, was now a bomb site, covered, as if in remembrance of bygone happier times, with clusters of rosebay willowherb, aptly nicknamed fireweed and little known in towns, since it sprung into life after the Great Fire of London.

Billy Lee's pub, the Traveller's Rest, had miraculously survived, although the buildings on either side had been destroyed. It was quite early, but I turned up Prince Street to seek a little solace in the Princess Hotel, headquarters of Sheffield Wednesday Supporters' Club. Behind the tiny bar the landlord, Bernard Parson, bald-headed and beaming, holder of the Military Medal from the Great War, broke off his conversation with a customer to serve me. The first pint of Richdale's tasted so good that I quickly followed it up with another. It was obvious as to where Mr Parson's loyalty lay, even if one was a stranger to the pub. The dial of the big clock had one half blue and the other white, as were the fingers. Photos of past Wednesday teams had frames of blue; behind the bar boxes of Scottish Bluebell matches instead of the usual red and white Captain Webb.

Nature called and I went outside in the yard to the gents. Two dustbins were painted white with blue lids, the walls striped in the same colours, as was the lavatory door. Alehouse gossip, usually reliable, had it that Bernard once refused to have a new gas meter fitted, because it was the detested red, until he'd painted it with his beloved Wednesday colours.

Bidding my genial host good night, I walked back down to The Moor. The Pump Tavern on the corner of Earl Street still breathed defiance, but opposite to it, where once had stood the fine buildings of Roberts Bros, Atkinson's, and Marks and Spencer, all that remained now were deep basements, half filled with water, surrounded by fences of wooden pales. Sometimes, after heavy rain, gangs of kids larked about in these makeshift swimming pools, paddling and splashing each other with the evil-smelling sludge. Williams' Deacons' bank at the corner of Rockingham Street was boarded up, mercifully covering the damage it had suffered. A little further along, past windowless and roofless shops, Binns', where I had been 'britched', and rumour had it that before the blitz it had been filled with cheap coffins ready for air raid casualties, was no more. On the other side of the road, the Devonshire Arms had suffered a like fate. All in all, as I stood there in the gathering gloom with not a light to be seen, it was a desolate setting, doing little to alleviate the melancholia that still lingered from my shattered romantic interlude. I thought that another dose of John Barleycorn's panacea for such a condition might be beneficial, so I ascended the wide wooden stairs to the concert room of the Grapes at the Moorhead.

What a contrast from the bleak, bomb-shattered streets! A long smoke-filled, brightly-lit room was packed with soldiers, sailors, airmen, ATS, WAAFs and American GIs. At the far end, on a small stage, a dinner-jacketed orchestra of elderly men supported the vocalist, Mary Miller, as she bravely trilled away, fighting a losing battle over the babble of voices. I pushed my way through to the bar and got a pint of Tennant's, feeling out of place in civvies: practically all the ones not in uniform were old men and local girls. The soft American drawl and posh southern accents contrasted strangely with the strung-together Sheffield dialect. Next to me, two women, both in their late twenties, puffed nervously at cigarettes, constantly flicking ash, both jabbering at the same time, but seemingly able to understand each other. One of them, whose hair was so dark it looked as though she had used black lead on it, appeared to have a grievance over her salary, chattering, ''E said, arlgithi ninepence a gross. Tha waint ar sed, a bob or nowt. Arlgooup t' tenpence, he sez. Ar telled 'im weer to purrit. Ar sed ar cud mek moor at back o' Fosters on a bad neet!' Her friend, with a chalk-white face, enlivened by vivid twin patches of rouge and pencilled eyebrows, also had her troubles, and started speaking before her companion had finished. 'Ar wor up from two o'clock other mornin' wi' babby teethin' an' t'other one wi diarrhoea an 'oopin' cough. Ar 'ad t' be at work fer six, mi Mam cum in from next door at five t' look after 'em. As soon as shop oppens, she said she'd get three penn'orth o' loddlum. Little buggers wor still bang art when ar gorrooam at hafe past two.'

They appeared to be desirous of company. Although the chatter continued unabated, both were obviously on the lookout. I finished my beer and was on the point of ordering another, wondering whether I dare ask them to have a drink. As a preliminary, I grinned at the one facing me, in what I thought was an agreeable manner. She gave me a look as cold as a lavatory pan in winter, then smiled dazzlingly at two big Yanks who were pushing through the crowd. 'Yoo hoo!' she squealed, delightedly. I made way for them at the bar, bidding the ladies a courteous good night, which was ignored, although I did overhear one remark to the other as I passed them, 'Y' get some funny buggers in 'eer nar. It din't used t'be like this befoor waar.' Pondering on this and wondering if they could possibly be alluding to me, I descended the stairs and wended my way across the Moorhead under the statue of Victory, guarded by twin cannon, and entered the Nelson. Here again, blinking in the brightness after the blacked-out street, all was music and light: a tinkling piano, Billy Malkin singing, and, inbetween, rousing melodies on the organ. I had another pint of bitter, Tennant's again, and began to survey the world in a slightly more benign manner. The beer gave me the courage, as I left the Nelson, to go up Cambridge Street and enter Nell's Bar. I had never been in this well-known hostelry, as I had always thought, judging by its flashy exterior of red and black vitriolite with chrome trim, that it was too posh for me.

Inside it was much quieter than the two previous pubs, but very comfortable, with leather chairs and seating around black marble-topped tables. I had a swift half of draught Bass, then went next door into the Gents' Bar to see what it was like. Smaller than the lounge, a few men were seated at tables and just one man standing at the bar. He turned as I entered, and gave me the only friendly smile I had received all evening. I ordered a Bass, feeling quite a man of the world in such exclusive surroundings, although I dropped some of the change, due to the clumsiness of the barman, or perhaps because the floor had become rather unsteady. Even so, I felt in top form, quickly downed my drink and asked for another.

Once again there was some difficulty with the money. I had taken a handful of coins from my pocket and was attempting to proffer the correct sum by paying them out one at a time on the bar. For some reason, the dispenser of drinks appeared very impatient, which didn't help me in my calculations. Halfway through the transaction, the friendly man said, 'Take it back, have this one on me.' At first I demurred, but he insisted. The barman heaved a sigh of relief, pushed back my money and rather rudely, I thought, plonked a glass of beer in front of me. My new-found friend and benefactor waved aside my profuse thanks and asked me, 'Have you been in here before? I don't remember seeing you.' He seemed very pleasant, but I wished that he would keep still. His face had a strange habit of appearing quite near and then moving out of focus. On the close-ups he was a man of about fifty, sleekly grey-haired, although his eyebrows and pencil-thin moustache were black. His voice was rather high-pitched and when he patted the back of my hand, his was soft and smooth.

He seemed genuinely interested when I told him, as if I were used to drinking and town life, 'I like to get off early if I fancy a pub crawl. It's no use starting when half the night's gone.' When I told him this, and informed him where I had been during the evening and how much I had had to drink, he gave a little whistle of admiration and declared, 'Well, I wouldn't believe it, you look as sober as a judge. Now take me, four halves of Bass and I'm anybody's!' Steadying the bar, I produced a ten bob note and called, 'Lesh 'av another.' The churlish barman, for some reason, appeared doubtful about serving me, but a nod from my

101

companion spurred him into action and I imposed my superiority by insisting that he too must have a drink. The amount of change he gave back seemed curiously light, but his manner was now deferential, as he raised a glass and wished me, 'Good health. My respects, sir.'

Aubrey — we had exchanged names by now — asked me if I was married, and when I replied in the negative became very attentive and declared, 'Tell you what, George, we'll have a special drink to celebrate our meeting.' He leaned over and whispered something to the barman, who looked round furtively, then, from under the counter, after a few mysterious movements, produced what looked like two glasses of water. I was in complete command of myself, but I must have looked puzzled, because Aubrey said, 'It's gin and tonic, a special favour to me — there's not much of it about.' I tried to give him the impression that it was one of my favourite tipples, when in actual fact I had never before tasted spirits, except for a teaspoonful of whisky at Christmas. It certainly went down very well, although I spilt a few drops when I missed my mouth because the building lurched. 'You ever been married, Aubrey?' I remarked casually, squinting at him and wondering why he kept swaying. He took a delicate sip of his drink, produced a packet of Craven A, put two in his mouth, lit them both and gave me one before replying, 'No, I'd rather go through life wanting something I hadn't got, instead of having something I didn't want!' This, to me, was the wittiest thing that I had ever heard, and I laughed heartily, took a swig of G and T, then a deep drag at my fag, which nearly choked me.

Aubrey patted my back solicitously until I recovered, then squeezed my arm, put his mouth close to my ear and murmured, 'What about coming over to my place? I've got a nice little flat in Cross Burgess Street. We can have a drink or two and a bit of supper.' This sounded OK to me. I was flattered that someone so distinguished and much older than me could make so generous an offer. As we left, I made a

magnanimous gesture of farewell to my friend behind the bar, knocked over a glass that some fool had put at my elbow, carefully avoided several stools and a table that were in the way, and, escorted by Aubrey, made for the door. It opened before we got there, and through the blackout curtain Moxay entered. It was good to see him. I thought that it was great that just after making a new friend an old one had appeared. I grasped him jocularly by the shoulders to keep him steady, but his welcoming grin disappeared as he saw my companion.

Remembering my manners, I introduced them. 'Albert, thish is Aubrey. I'm goin' back to his place for a bit o' supper.' 'Dar not,' Albert tersely replied. Then, eyeing Aubrey grimly, he snapped 'Piss off!' 'Juss a minit,' I remonstrated, but Aubrey gave me a sickly smile, did as he had been requested, and vanished into the night. Moxay guided me to a table, went up to the bar and came back with two glasses of beer. 'Wot's up?' I said plaintively, 'I was just ready for a bit o' supper.' Moxay eyed me good-humouredly. 'Dar'd a got moor dan a bit o' supper if dar'd a gone back wi 'im. Dunt dar know 'oo 'e is?' I shook my head emphatically from side to side. Albert tut-tutted at my ignorance. ''E's an owd puff — 'e's allus after young blokes. 'E tried it on wi' me once int Athol, an' ar lerrim think 'e wor on to a good thing, 'til we gorrartside, den ar kneed 'im in 'bollocks.'

I looked admiringly at Moxay — he always seemed to me to be master of any situation — and asked him to have another drink. He declined, explaining that he had just nipped out for a quick one and had to get back to his fire watching post because he'd booked in a Yank and lady friend in five minutes' time. We parted outside Nell's. He marched briskly up Cambridge Street and I set off on my travels. There was something strange about the pavement, because it kept rising up before I had completed a stride, which made my progress somewhat erratic, and even more so when gas lamps and heaps of sandbags suddenly moved into my path. The Angel beckoned invitingly, but I resisted her charms and continued on my meandering way along Button Lane. Someone was singing quite loudly and it was only when 'and the waters as they flow, seem to murmur sweet and low, you are my heart's desire, I love you, Nellie Dean!' came round for a second time that I realised that I was the singer, which made me laugh no end. I tacked across Fitzwilliam Street. Some idiot in a motor car with dimmed headlamps tooted his horn and swerved across my path, before disappearing into the blackout. 'It's a good job I'm a bit nippy on the old feet,' I congratulated myself, 'or he would have had me.' A smell of chips frying tickled my taste buds, luring me into Mucky Emma's chip 'oil. I pushed through the blackout curtain into the welcoming blue smoke and heat from the coal fire which the proprietress was stoking. I ordered a penn'orth of chips with some scraps, which quickly appeared on the counter.

I tried a chip and decided the rest would be improved by a little salt. It must have been damp. Nothing came out of the big aluminium salt pot, even though I shook it vigorously, so I banged it hard on the counter top and tried again, this time so successfully that the lid came off and the entire contents of the canister landed on my chips. Mumbling an apology and deciding not to bother with any vinegar, I slunk out. At the corner of Thomas Street, I gulped down my alfresco supper, screwed up the paper and flung it into the Iron Duke. Someone must have been inside obeying the call of nature, because a voice shouted out enquiring, 'Wot the bloody 'ell y' playin' at?' This appeal, salt on my lips and a thick layer of grease on the roof of my mouth, urged me up the two steps which I found a little tricky to climb. After the glamour of the town watering holes, the little back-street pub was too quiet, so I quickly guzzled down a pint, which, for some reason, the landlord seemed reluctant to serve me. I made another perilous descent down the steps, the last one giving enough impetus to carry me across the street into the Vine. Once again, mine host eyed me rather suspiciously as he pulled a pint. 'Wot's wrong wi' everybody t'night?' I thought. 'I'm alright an' my money's as good as anyone else's.' I giggled at someone facing me from another room across the bar. His hair stood on end, his collar and tie had slipped halfway round a long thin neck and the eyes, unnaturally brilliant, sometimes stared vacantly at me. He seemed to have some difficulty in standing upright, and I had to laugh when his elbow slipped off the bar, making him disappear for a moment.

I had a good swig of beer and so did he. When I picked my nose, he did likewise. Finishing my drink, I decided to have another, so in an attempt to attract someone's attention, I banged down my pint pot firmly on the bar. I must have gained some power from the chips because the glass shattered, leaving the handle gripped in my hand. This feat of strength impressed me so much that I stared fixedly at the fragments, unable to believe what had happened. Suddenly, at the side of my friend, the landlord appeared. I grinned at him, but somehow he looked very grim. My hearing was quite acute because, although he was in the other room, his voice was loud in my ear, as he ordered me, 'Cum on, thee, outside, thar's 'ad enuff!' A firm hand on the scruff of my neck propelled me and my chum out of the pub and into the darkened street. It was so black after the brightness of the alehouse that I couldn't see him. After a tentative call or two with no answer, I shrugged my shoulders and decided to go home. The railings of the infant school where I had started my educational career so many years ago gave me a little support, until I turned down Headford Street and the pavement started moving again. I decided to stand outside the blacked-out Moxay household for a little while. In spite of her apparent rejection of me, I felt that with only a brick wall between us at least I was near to her. A wave of loneliness and an intense longing for a glimpse of Molly came over me, so strongly that I picked up a small pebble and lobbed it up to an upstairs window which, in my highly emotional state, I fancied was my beloved's boudoir.

No response, so I tried again with a larger stone. Lurching about though I was, my aim was sure and I hit the target with a fair crack. The casement was flung open, my yearning heart gave a tremendous leap of expectation, then dropped like a brick as instead of the mellifluous sound of Molly's voice the strident tones of her mother screeched through

the merciful concealing darkness, 'Get thissen off, daft bugger!' This request was followed up by a shower of liquid, which, although some of it missed me, the fragance of the rest, which didn't, made me aware that it was the contents of a chamber pot. My ardour dampened, I slowly made my way along Moore Street, only the occasional meeting with a wall to keep me company. After a few yards it became increasingly evident that a turbulent battle was being fought in my stomach. A series of heavy nauseous attacks culminated in a wave of bitter bile gushing up my throat and out of the mouth, bearing on it the beer, gin and salty chips of my evening's entertainment. Bent almost double as I was, the flow seemed never-ending until at last the rumblings and retching finally ceased and I could straighten up to wipe my mouth and watering eyes. In a brief interlude of clarity following this upheaval, I became suddenly aware that I was standing on the very spot where Molly so recently had been overcome by just such a sentimental spasm as I had undergone. A few words by Thomas Hardy shone through the maudlin mist: 'A sign that they were bent by paths coincident, on being anon twin halves of one august event.' In this mawkish mood, which soon evaporated as stupor returned, I reached our front door. The keyhole seemed unable to keep still, and after a few poking near misses, I finally did effect an entrance. In spite of my caution, Mother, ever on the alert for the return of her prodigal son, called down from the bedroom, 'Is that you, Georgie?' I mumbled an affirmation, took off my shoes in the living room and made the perilous ascent up the stairs. The buttons on my shirt took so much time to undo, and awkward collar studs which baffled my fumbling fingers proved such an obstacle, that I abandoned the attempt and flopped on top of the bed, still trousered and wearily waited for soothing slumber.

I didn't rest very long in the arms of Morpheus. Instead, the room started to spin round and round ever faster and I had to hold on to the sides of the mattress in case I was flung out of bed. If I opened my eyes the spinning slowed down, only to start up again when I closed them.

All through the night, I was riding on a mad merry-go-round in the company of Moxay, narky landlords, Mucky Emma, the owd puff, and at my side rode Molly, tantalisingly close, but as I reached out for her, she simpered, tossed those flaming locks and was gone. It was always the same, until finally, as if our time on the crazy carousel was up, it came to a standstill and my companions vanished. I drifted into a troubled sleep, to be rudely awakened minutes later by Dad calling, 'Get up Georgie, you'll be late for work, it's seven o'clock.' Wearily, I sat on the edge of the bed, holding a head that throbbed like the beat of a muffled drum at a royal funeral, licking parched lips with a tongue coated in dry sawdust, and made an eternal vow: 'Never again.'

Chapter 22

Matters Military

*I*HAD SERVED in the Home Guard for well over a year and in that time had been trained to use the rifle and bayonet, Sten gun and the Vickers machine gun. The snag was that I had never actually fired a shot and the only thing I had ever bayoneted was a sandbag suspended from a rope. There seemed to be hope of some action when Sergeant Major Gibson informed us that our platoon was to march up to the rifle range near the Nunnery Colliery on the Manor for firing practice. We arrived there in a state of excited anticipation, which increased as we unloaded from a lorry boxes of 303 ammunition and stacks of rifles. I was a bit deflated when myself and Big Okker, along with some other privates, were assigned to target duty. This entailed standing in a deep trench behind the target and signalling each hit with a board on the end of a long pole.

After a while it became a trifle onerous, because most of the shots were off course, thudding into the clayey bank behind us, therefore not requiring any signal. It was a relief when, after an hour of this inactivity, we were recalled to the firing positions, filled with eager expectation of having a pop. Not long before, I had seen a film at the Star, titled *Sergeant York*, in which Gary Cooper played a Quaker who reluctantly joined the United States Army in the Great War, became a crackshot and killed hundreds of Jerries.

I pictured myself wetting a thumb and calmly touching the foresight of my rifle, just as he had done, then banging home one bullseye after another. We lined up in front of Gibby, impatient to get started. 'Well done lads,' he said, looking pleased, although I thought I could detect

a hint of malevolence in his eyes. 'Lieutenant Finch has ordered me to tell you that we're comin' up 'ere every week in summer.' Here he paused, waiting for the murmur of approbation to quieten down. 'There's summat else ar've got t' tell yer.' Again a pause, until a frosty smile lightened his soldierly features and he continued, 'Owin' t' short supply of ammo, there was only enuff fer officers an' NCOs. Sorry lads, better luck next week. Fall art an' tek five.'

With this, he marched off, his grin broadening all the while. Okker looked at me in disbelief as the gallant soldier strode away to join the group of jovial 'marksmen'. 'Short supply!' he snorted, 'Thi's abart a ton o' bloody lead in dat bleedin' bank side. Sumdy'll mek a fortune diggin' it art after waar!' Two nights later I reported for duty at the drill hall to find a little band of my comrades gathered in front of the notice board. On it, a terse official communication stated that all Home Guard personnel under the age of forty who worked regular day shifts would be posted to the Somme Barracks on Glossop Road for training on rocket gun anti-aircraft batteries. This was more like it, I thought, better than a piffling Sten or a rifle, and also with the threat of invasion fading away, probably the last chance to have a bash at the Boche.

My first taste of rocket projector training took place one evening in a large wooden shed, occupying a corner of the barrack yard. A Royal Artillery Sergeant called Bradshaw, too old for active service, gave a brief outline about the functions of the projector outside, then marched us into the shed, where in the middle of the sand-covered floor stood our answer to the bomber. He eyed some of us rather dubiously, especially me, I thought, when he stated that all gun crews had to have good eyesight and be physically fit, so as to be able to set the fuses accurately and lift the heavy projectiles. I realised what he meant as we underwent our first drill. Each rocket was about six feet long, four inches in diameter and made of thick, heavy sheet metal. The sharp end culminated in a twelve-inch-long high-explosive shell, with a time fuse in the nose cone. Sergeant Bradshaw made the demonstration look quite simple, acting as loader whilst an experienced gunner operated the controls. The procedure was to extract, grasping its stabilising fins, the rocket from the loading rack, drop the projectile onto one's left forearm, run over to the projector, slide the missile

up the guide rails, then pull it smartly back to engage the electrical firing contacts. Most of our chaps had no difficulty with the unwieldy missiles, especially Okker, who handled them as if they were cricket stumps. I had been watching carefully and when my turn came stepped forward confidently, grasped the fins firmly, pulled the rocket sharply from its rack and dropped it smartly on my forearm, which gave way under the weight, allowing the projectile to embed itself in the ground at an angle of thirty degrees.

In the silence that followed, I tried desperately, but without success, to rectify my error, until the sergeant stepped forward, got hold of the rocket with one hand, pulled it out of the ground and replaced it in the rack. He was quite understanding and showed his appreciation of my predicament by informing me and everyone else, including people outside in Glossop Road, shouting, 'Y' big tart, gie o'er playin' wi' it, tha'll gu blind. Tell thi mother t' mek thi sum beef tea!' I bit my lip, and tried again. The knack was to drop the rocket a lot nearer its nose cone onto the arm. Once I became proficient, I found the life of a gunner, albeit part-time, enjoyable, and looked forward to the nights at the Somme, even guard duty. One night, standing outside the big wooden gates, performing this assignment, I reflected on how my military status had improved since I was a raw recruit at the drill hall. Now, I had a uniform and greatcoat that fitted me, and a steel helmet that nearly did, and instead of a pick shaft held a Lee Enfield rifle, admittedly unloaded. My garters and boots were as bright as any Coldstream's, and all in all, though never blooded in combat as yet, I felt capable of coping with any emergency or battle situation that might arise.

The street was very quiet. A tram, its dim blue lights already on in the twilight, cruised slowly up to Crookes. A few passers-by mooched aimlessly about, a couple pausing to look in Jamesons's windows, one of the rare shops with anything to display. A few lines, remembered from somewhere, came to me and I straightened my back and shoulders, assuming a proud military posture, as I whispered, 'The Guards die but do not surrender!' I heard the clicking of high heels coming down Gell Street, and, ever on the alert, without turning my head I looked sideways and beheld, coming towards me, two females. One of them had been pointed out to me in town as the well-endowed figure of a lady of the night known as 'California Rose' — maybe because of the perfume that she obviously so lavishly applied, or her complexion, which was decidedly florid. Her hair was blond and long, her skirt tight and short as she clicked towards me, her hips swaying provocatively. At her side, the younger woman, undoubtedly her protégé, tried to emulate her mentor, although with the advantage of youth on her side she had little need. Rose, not wasting a professional glance on me, swayed past, her delicate yet somehow irresistibly enticing natural odour of woman, enhanced by cheap scent, titillated and aroused my masculine desires. Her companion, to my surprise, instead of accompanying her stopped in front of me. She couldn't have been more than eighteen, but heavy make-up, lipstick and mascara made her look older. Her moist red lips parted and she breathed heavily, her ample bosom heaving beneath her tightly-stretched blouse as she pressed close to me and murmured seductively, 'Have you got the time, soldier?' Before I had a chance to look at my wristwatch, Rose came marching back, and seizing her pupil by an arm cried laughingly, 'Cum on, silly bitch, stop playin' abart, 'e's not a proper sojer, 'e's ony a bleedin' Home Guard!' As they clicked away, giggling into the gathering dusk, I shouted after them, 'It's about twenty past nine,' a piece of helpful information that for some reason brought on shrieks of laughter from the provocative pair.

Geo. Cunningham

Chapter 23

The Big Race Day

MY CAREER as a die-sinker was, to say the least, a trifle disorganised. Harry Benton, now in his late sixties, was a sick man. Some days he did more coughing and expectorating than die-sinking, although his good humour never flagged. The periods he had to stay away from work varied from odd days to weeks at a time, so when this happened I was in charge of the die shop and the betting slips. Born in 1876, Harry was one of the old school of Victorian craftsmen who had never moved with the times. All the machining and surface grinding of the steel blocks was done at James Bros, a small engineering firm in Trafalgar Street. I soon evolved quite a good system on Harry's off days.

The first two or three hours of the morning were employed in working on a die until the betting slips started to come in. 'Mac' Coles was an invaluable assistant and advisor to me, especially on big race days. He was a spoon and fork stamper, and so expert at his job that he invariably had a copy of the *Daily Herald* opened at the racing pages beside him on his drop stamp. The hammer was operated by a foot pedal, and Mac could pick out his horses and decide on what bets to have whilst still stamping, never once making a waster.

On Derby day I put all the slips and money into a paper bag, picked up two heavy blocks of steel due for machining and set off along Bath Street. It was a beautiful sunny morning and, in spite of the weighty dies, I was glad to escape from the factory. As evidence of the race's importance, a little queue of old men and one or two women had gathered up to Fred Harrison, each of them wanting to make sure that their money was on. I stood at the end of the line, enjoying the sunshine and good-humoured remarks. A stout woman, whom I knew as Mrs Giddings, robed in a coverall, a sacking apron and plimsolls, had just said impatiently, 'Cum on, shek thissen, ar've got mar mester's dinner t' purron,' when suddenly, without warning, Fred, who always had one eye for the money and the other for his touts, turned abruptly and shot up the entry. Everyone except me seemed to know just what to do. The men, old though they were, hobbled at a fair lick after the fleeing bookie, and the women disappeared quickly into nearby houses, leaving me, weighted down as I was, alone in the deserted street.

There I stood, gawping, wondering what was happening, when behind me a door opened and a firm hand clutched my arm and dragged me inside a house. The door was quickly slammed behind me and a rough voice growled, 'Wot wor tha standin' theer for like souse? Dusta tha wanta t' get pinched?' The closed curtains in the little front room made it dark and hazardous for me after the brightness outside, and all I could do was obey my rescuer when he ordered, 'Put them dies on' flooer an' cum wi' me.' I did as I was told and stumbled after him, bumping into furniture, then through a door in a living room. Around a large scrubbed table, industriously plying knives and forks with every sign of enjoying a cooked dinner, were seated a man and a woman, also without hat and coat. The man was Fred Harrison. Before I had the chance to ask him what he was doing, the woman quickly fetched two plates from a cupboard, and just as quickly filled them with steaming hash from a large stewpot.

My host plonked me down in a chair beside him, and I mechanically started to eat. None of the people seemed a bit surprised at my sudden

appearance at the table, but carried on eating and talking as if an unexpected guest was an everyday occurrence. Fred was in good spirits, bestowing on me a mysterious knowing wink inbetween mouthfuls of food. I had never before seen him without a raincoat and trilby and I was about to enquire if he, like me, had been dragged in for lunch, when suddenly, in the open door facing me, appeared two very large men. Both were clad in dirty oil-stained boiler suits and wore bicycle clips. I felt a sudden jolt of recognition which I tried to conceal. What were they doing dressed like this? I asked myself, as I confirmed that they were two usually smartly uniformed local constables, who languished under the nicknames of 'Tashy' and 'Knock-Knock'. It was apparent that they had recently been performing some strenuous exercise, as both of them were panting for breath and sweating profusely.

'Knock-Knock', so called from his habit of knocking on walls with his truncheon, gaped in disbelief as he beheld Fred, who with every sign of enjoyment, was obviously employed in finishing a plateful of hash, using a large crust of bread to mop up the gravy. The constable pointed an accusing finger at him and gasped, 'Ar saw you teckin bets at bottom o' entry a minute since!' 'Nay, nay!' cried the lady, whom I took to be our hostess, ''E's bin 'ere a gud hafe 'our. Sithee, 'ee's nearly finished 'is dinner an' ar gerrim a reight dollop.' 'Tashy', whose large hairy appendage under the nose had labelled him with his moniker, glared at me and snapped, 'Ooa you?' I sat, petrified, fear depriving me of speech, but the lady's husband quickly answered, ''E works at Viner's, a pal o' mine from theer sent 'im on wi' a jar o' red cabbage.' Fortunately, on the table stood the irrefutable evidence, and I marvelled at the quick-wittedness of my table companion. The constables, baffled by the bland unconcern of the dinner party, withdrew, but not before 'Knock-Knock', red-faced and furious, snarled, 'Ar'll 'av you yet, Fred, just see if I don't!' With this Parthian shot, they plodded across the yard and went up the double entry.

I was still mystified as to where Mr Harrison's hat and raincoat were, until the cellar head door opened and out came a young woman carrying the garments. Her eyes alighted on the plate that Fred was polishing to a very high finish. 'Y' greedy bugger!' she cried, 'Ar 'ope thar enjoyed mar dinner.' However, she was quickly mollified by a two bob piece from the bookie, who also gave the same to her mother. The man, a large bald-headed individual, who had dragged me in from the street, got up from the table and said, 'Gi 'em five minutes, then tha can gerroff. It's a good job ar spotted thi artside. Ar'm a pal o' Harry Benton's an' ar've seen thee bringin' bets befoor, an' when them coppers were spotted, ar pulled thi in ar 'ouse.' 'But, how did you know that they were bobbies?' I queried. He sucked his few remaining teeth as if I were insulting his intelligence. 'Easy,' he replied, lighting a Woodbine. 'They got sum mucky overalls an' rode up Headford Street on bikes, but owd China Hudson wor pikin' off artside Dog an' Gun. 'E soon spotted 'em an' gen us wire.' It was evident to my rescuer that I still couldn't understand how the bobbies' disguise had been detected until he carried on. 'They were tryin' t' mek thessens look like workmen, wi' boiler suits an' all, but nobody's ever seen a nobber wi' polished black boots 'av thi? Owd China soon twigged 'em.'

After a cautionary look outside, satisfying myself that the coast was clear, I resumed my errand to James Bros, left the steel blocks, picked up a pair of machined dies and returned whence I came. A little bow-legged man lurked at the bottom of the bookie's entry, stuffing betting slips and money into his pockets. He stopped me and muttered, 'Ar'm standin' in fer Fred 'til things cool darn. When thar brings bets temorra, gie 'em ter me, awright?' When I got back to the factory, I related to Mac the story of my betting run.

I was still full of admiration for the ingenuity of Bath Street people. He chuckled and said, 'Tha knows wot thi say, Georgie, "If tha catches a weasel asleep, piss in its ear!"' Mac was in high spirits next morning.

He exclaimed, when he brought in the betting slips, 'It's a good job them coppers din't nab owd Fred, ar think everybody in Bath Street an' Sheffield backed big winner. Ar wun a few bob missen.' When I enquired what had won, he looked at me in amazement. 'Dun't da know, it wor Harry Wragg on Watling Street. Thi don't call 'im 'ead waiter fer nowt, he waits at back, keepin' arta rooad, den 'e cums past 'em like a train.' Influenced by Mac's knowledge of racing, I put a tanner each way on a dead cert that he tipped, which came in last of a field of twenty runners.

Chapter 24

The Beer Poacher

SLOWLY, the fourth year of the war dragged on. To celebrate my nineteenth birthday, Mam bought me a Tootal tie costing one and six-pence, and the RAF bombed Naples. The Russians were doing well, counter-attacking on all fronts. Italy did a complete turnaround and declared war on Germany.

The tremendous events and battles taking place worldwide filled the newspapers, and the general feeling was that at long last the tide was turning in our favour. All this faded into insignificance one night, when, turning the pages of the *Telegraph*, a tiny paragraph overshadowed everything. In a few lines it stated, 'Sergeant, Air-Gunner, Vincent Crookes, missing in a raid on Hanover, October 18th/19th.' The same age as me, nineteen, a hero of many bombing raids, had given his all for his country and what had I done? I stared at the print in disbelief, thinking of the last time I saw Vinny, as he waved goodbye.

The autumn, as if in sympathy, was dull and grey and early in December it snowed. I felt the need to get out of town, if only for a few hours, so one Saturday afternoon I boarded a Fulwood tram outside the Stores in Ecclesall Road. The dirty slosh of the city was transformed into an unsullied fairyland as the tram groaned and clanged higher and higher. I was the only passenger occupying the top deck on that bitterly cold winter afternoon. My thoughts went back to that summer's day when Vinny, Norman and I mounted that exciting expedition to the crags. Then the trees were full-leafed and green, the sky was blue and birds sang. Now, against a leaden sky, branches stood out stark and bare and a few rooks cawed raucously. I got off the tram at the terminus alongside Fulwood Church and trudged through the steadily falling snow up onto the drains. This narrow conduit ran from the dams at Redmires and conveyed water to a covered reservoir at Carsick Hill. The bank was also a convenient footpath which our intrepid trio had discovered.

I started to enjoy the walk, in spite of the weather, even though up past the top of Crimicar Lane the snow was drifting knee deep. Onward, ever onward I ploughed, not a living soul in sight on that lonely trail. Over to my left huddled Peat Farm, sheltering under dog-legged Roper Hill, its near neighbours Racecourse Farm and Soughley black against the white fields. I was glad to reach Soughley Lane and turn into Redmires Road and get the north-west wind behind me.

No one was about; the deep snow was unbroken, not a footstep or a wheel-mark marred its surface. The high stone wall surrounding the camp, which was built for our troops, now detained prisoners of war. A sentry at his post in a box near the gates became alert as I approached, but relaxed and said 'Ar do' as I passed him. A light came on in a window at Mons Villas, only to be quickly covered by a blackout blind, even though it was early afternoon. I hesitated at the Three Merry Lads, but decided to push on to the Sportsman. The only sign of life in the bleak landscape was smoke streaming horizontally from the chimney of the little stone-built Hope Cottage across the road from the pub. Thankfully, as I knocked off the snow from my boots on the doorstep of the Sportsman and tried the door, it was open.

Three or four men were in the dram shop to the right, basking in the warmth of a big log fire which blazed in a dog grate. The landlord, Fred Bonnington, fair-haired and jovial, wearing a waistcoat and in his

Geo. Cunningham

REDMIRES ROAD

SPORTSMAN INN
J. NICHOLSON

Geo. Cunningham

shirt sleeves, looked at me quizzically when I asked for a pint, but must have decided I was of age and served me from a tiny bar. One of the men, obviously a regular, called out 'Bring me one an' all, Fred, while tha't theer.' I sat in a corner, glad of the warmth and feeling rather sleepy after a few drinks of beer. In fact, I had to check myself from nodding off, no doubt as the result of a couple of nights fire watching. Suddenly the outer door opened, a man, capped and overcoated rushed in, bringing with him a flurry of snowflakes and an icy draught. Before anybody had a chance to remonstrate about this untimely intrusion, the man shouted, 'Jerries are cummin!' Half asleep as I was, I jerked upright, automatically reaching for my rifle. Was this it? Had the Germans finally invaded? How could I get back to the barracks, or, better still, Michael Road?

Precedence of age forgotten in this startling moment, I crowded with the men into the bay window. Wiping away the steam with our bare hands — although in his haste to see the enemy one of the men used his cap — we gazed down the road. Through the greyness of the winter's afternoon and driving snow slowly appeared two British soldiers, in full battle order, shouldering rifles. We gave a nervous laugh, but the messenger cried, ''Owd on a bit, Jerries are behind 'em. Coaches which brought 'em from railway station 'av all got stuck in a drift near 'ospital gates, so guards are marchin' 'em up t' camp.' So it was; shepherded by our troops, a long line of prisoners stumbled along the snowy road to captivity. I left the pub to get a better look at the enemy, my first sight of the vaunted Wehrmacht in four years of war. After the warmth of the pub, it felt colder than ever outside as I hunched my shoulders against the bitter wind.

The column of about forty men passed me quite closely, some of them trying to put on an air of arrogance, but most of them looked dejected and downfallen, clutching little bundles of personal possessions. I was surprised that a few of them were youngsters, not as old as me; in fact one or two were mere schoolboys. A little group, banded together in the last days of comradeship, were sun-bronzed and still wore the long peaked cap of the Africa Corps, ideal in the desert heat but not much cop on a winter's day at Redmires. These then were the men, or what was left of them, who had conquered all in their path and made their Führer, Hitler, ruler of Europe from the Arctic to the Mediterranean. I was about to go back into the Sportsman when one of the prisoners turned his head and stared bleakly at me, a momentary insolent flicker in his blue eyes quenched by hopelessness as he trudged on to prison, and for him, the end of conquests.

There was something vaguely familiar about him, even in such a brief glimpse. Tall and well built, even though his shoulders were bowed in defeat, those eyes and cropped flaxen hair convinced me that he was

Helmut Hegner. A bit different from a sunny sea cruise with the Strength through Joy movement, I thought, as I watched the melancholy figures fade away into the barren, snow-swept waste of Lodge Moor. Pondering about the vagaries of life's fortunes and thinking how lucky I was not to be in Helmut's position, I took my seat in the dram shop to discover that, whilst I had been outside for a few minutes, some kind soul had taken the opportunity to drink most of my beer. There wasn't much point in making any rash accusations, so I drank the little that was left and got another pint. It was so quiet and peaceful: the tick of the clock, an occasional low mutter from one of the men only served to intensify the silence. A long-haired collie lay stretched at the feet of his master, a grumpy-looking stumpy man, clad in corduroy, who looked to me as though he could be the beer poacher. He was smoking a cherry wood pipe — rather more matches than tobacco, judging by the amount of spent ones he dropped on the stone-flagged floor, sooner than making the effort to throw them in the fire.

From where I was sitting, I could see Lodge Moor Hospital and I got to thinking about the time, not so long ago, when I spent months behind those walls with only a slight chance of surviving, and yet here I was, supping ale, a stone's throw away from my erstwhile sickbed. A curious acrid smell suddenly began to pervade the room. Fred, the landlord, wrinkled his nose in distaste and poked the fire, but that didn't make any difference; in fact, if anything, the stink got worse. He went into the lounge and the rest of the pub, to come back and state, 'It's ony in 'eer, thi's nowt anyweer else.'

It was a mystery. Everyone was sniffing the air like retrievers until suddenly I noticed, rising from the matted hair of Grumpy's dog, a wisp of smoke. 'That's what it is!' I cried triumphantly, pointing an accusing finger at the unfortunate canine. Indeed it was so; its owner had carelessly dropped a lighted match onto man's best friend, which still lay there, sleeping soundly.

Fred reacted instantly. He grabbed Grumpy's pint pot and poured a liberal shower of beer onto the conflagration. The old dog, rudely aroused from his snooze, heaved himself upright and shook his shaggy coat vigorously, then looked up at his master with reproachful eyes. Grumpy, very annoyed as he held up his empty vessel, cried, 'Tha' better gi' mi another pint for nowt, Fred!'

'Likely,' said the landlord, 'Ar'm fed up wi' thee cummin' in 'eer, sittin' in best seat in 'ouse fer 'ours wi' one drink, an' throwin' matches all o'er shant, an' nar, t' top it all, tha set thi own dog on fire!' 'Right,' retorted Grumpy, 'Tha'll not see me in 'eer ageean.' 'Good,' quoth mine host, as the man and his dog made their exit, 'Never'll bi too soon!' We watched the pair as they departed down the road, struggling against the blizzard. Fred smiled with satisfaction as they went out of sight and returned to the fire, standing with his back to it, saying, 'I've bin waitin' a long time t' get shut on 'im. Ar'm sure 'e supped blokes' ale when thi went t' back.' It appeared then, that my suspicions had been well founded, as tranquillity returned once more to the tavern.

Chapter 25

The Eternal Triangle

I WAS WALKING up Clarence Street one dark January evening on my way to fire watching duty at Viner's, when a familiar voice hailed me from the doorway of a house in Milton Street. 'Ey up!' it called, 'Cum o'er 'eer will ta?' It was the dulcet tones of Mrs Gumson, who as I came closer said, 'Oh, it's thee Georgie. Ar din't know who it were in this blinkin' blackout.' The living room of the back-to-back house was darker than outside until Mrs Gumson lit a candle after carefully closing the door behind me. In its flickering light I could see the form of a man half laid in an armchair, with his head back and snoring loudly. 'It's a good job ar spotted thi, Georgie,' whispered the fair lady. 'Thi art next dooar, an at other side 'e's as deaf as a bloody 'addock.' She continued, 'Gas mantle's bust, ar'v gorra new un, jus purrit on fer me. Wi bein' s' tall tha can reach up better than me.'

I took the fragile inverted mantle from its cardboard container and carefully fitted it into the holder. I took the candle and pulled down a chain attached to the pipe. There was a faint hiss, a pungent smell of gas, a plop as it ignited, and the room was bathed in a warm, greeny-yellow light. 'That's better,' said Mrs Gumson quietly, 'Ar doan't know wot ar would a' done if ar an't seen you passin'. 'E's on mornins, an 'e's just 'ad 'is tea an' ar din't want ter wekken 'im,' indicating the man in the chair. He was in his fifties, very portly, his unbuttoned waistcoat revealing an expansive union flanelled stomach encircled by a wide leather belt, studded with army cap badges.

The heavy jowled face sported a large moustache which, as he exhaled after every snore, fluttered in the breeze like a banner. His hands, comfortably clasped over his stomach, were surprisingly white and hairless, as were his thick forearms. A large colourful tattoo on one of them intrigued me enough to take a closer look. It was the head and shoulders of a nude, coquettish-looking woman, flaunting her ample breasts. Behind her was a bottle of whisky and a hand of cards. In front, discreetly covering the rest of her charms, was an elaborate scroll bearing the inscription 'A man's ruin'.

'Ar, he's bin a bit of a lad in 'is time,' ejaculated Mrs Gumson, standing with head on one side, and arms folded, fondly regarding the reclining Romeo. ''E used t' 'av lasses queuing up t' dance wi' 'im. 'E could 'av 'is pick, an' then ar cum on scene an' stopped his capers.' She chuckled and stepped carefully over his feet to poke the fire, then lowered the clothes nearer to the heat. 'Ar like t' see 'is clooas aired. 'E's guin' to a Buff meetin' in Bath Hotel at eight o'clock an' ar don't want 'im ter catch cowd.' Bidding the matriarch farewell, I set off for Viner's, just up the road.

The threat of air raids seemed to have faded away, and discipline at the command post had become pretty relaxed. In fact, it was more like a select club, the difference being that the members, instead of subscribing, were paid to attend. About eight o'clock it was my turn to go out for half an hour. Squire Rogers, my usual companion, declined to accompany me, saying, 'Ar've got guts ache,' so I sallied forth alone into the dark streets. Not very far, though, because it was raining, so I strolled across Broomhall street to the Poplar Tavern. The dark-panelled and wooden-seated hostelry was presided over by Walter Wragg, uncle of Sheffield's famous jockey, Harry Wragg. He beamed at me as I came in, probably because, except for a couple in a corner of the best room, the place was empty. I stood at the tiny bar, which had the advantage of a good view into the two rooms that comprised the pub, and slowly drank a pint of Tennant's. It was so good I ordered another and decided to sit in the best room, which although dimly lit was warmer than the dram shop, which didn't have a fire.

The couple opposite me didn't look up as I entered and took a seat just inside the door behind the high side of the wooden land settle. They seemed engrossed in their own company, staring into each other's eyes, even when drinking. The woman's face was vaguely familiar, even in the shadowy room, and it was with a jolt of surprise that I recognised the fair features of Nellie Slatters, Mrs Gumson's best friend. Why I didn't know her at once was because she had a kiss curl, twin patches of rouge on her cheeks, lipstick and, at the side of the left eye, an alluring black beauty spot. A fur boa, which had seen better days, and even at my distance smelled strongly of mothballs, girdled her scrawny neck which protruded from a long blue coat. I was even more surprised when I turned my attention, trying not to be nosy, onto her gentleman companion.

It was most definitely Mr Gumson. His bowler hat, tipped to the back of the head for comfort, set off his florid face and bushy moustache to their full advantage. He was wearing a navy blue serge suit with the jacket open to display his manly waistcoated 'corporation', which was embellished by a silver Albert from which hung several medals. A full half of his beer disappeared in one swig, which brought a gasp of admiration from Nellie. 'Whew!' she exclaimed, before taking a demure sip of her shandy, 'Y' can't half knock 'em back, Oliver, it's no wonder y' looks well. Ar wish my owd man'd tek a drink or two, it might liven 'im up a bit.'

Mr Gumson, enjoying the adulation, squeezed her hand, his moustache fluttering as he enquired, 'Weer is 'e t'neet? Wot did tha tell 'im when tha cum art?' Nellie giggled. 'Tha woulda laughed. 'E likes t' go t' bed early, ar don't know fer what, an' 'e allus warms a fire brick in oven an' puts it in an owd sock t' tek upstairs and shove it in bed.' She paused for a sip and a dab of her hanky before continuing. 'When feet in 'is socks are too far gone t' darn any moor, a cut 'em off an' knit a new un on. Well, I amt 'ad time t' do any knittin', an' ar forgot t' tell 'im, so 'e put bloody brick in leg an it dropped straight darn, reight on 'is tooars!' I thought Oliver was going to have a fit, he laughed so much. 'Ar towd 'im ar were guin' t' Mothers' Union at Chapel, an' ar left 'im wi' 'is foot up on a chair,' said Nellie.

Oliver emptied his pint pot and took the lady's hand in his beefy paw as he tenderly asked her to ''Av summat a bit stronger, eh? 'Ar'll ask if thi've gorrenny sherry, y'know wot thi say, "Beer meks y' cheer, sherry meks y' merry". Ar daren't say wot brandy meks yer!' This sally brought forth a peal of laughter from Nellie in which Oliver freely joined, pleased at the effect of this original witticism. He lumbered out of the room, not even bestowing a look on me and returned with a pint of beer and a baby Guinness. 'Sorry luv, no sherry, it's ony a beer 'ouse,' he apologised, sitting closer to the seductress and squeezing her arm. 'Any rooad, "Guinness for strength",' he quoted. 'Appen it'll bi me that needs it before neet's art, eh?' They both chortled at this, Nellie blushing a little beneath the powder.

I felt a draught of coldness enter the room, and there, framed in the doorway, almost filling it, was the formidable figure of Mrs Gumson. One hand was clutching her body, roughly in the region where her heart beat, and from the other swung a quart jug. Oliver's mouth dropped open. His moustache, which seconds before had bristled with ardour, drooped limply and his eyes bulged like a terror-stricken rabbit. Nellie, too late, snatched her hand from Oliver's and put her fingers up to her lips as if to stifle a scream.

After an eternity of silence, Mr Gumson, as if mesmerised, or like someone waking from a bad dream, cleared his throat and in a strangled voice croaked weakly, ''Ello luv, what are you doin' 'ere?' This innocuous remark, probably the only thing he could think of saying in the circumstances, ignited the powder keg of his wife's emotions. 'Wot am I doin' 'ere?' came the opening shot of the barrage. She paused to let it sink in. 'Ar'll tell y' wot ar'm doin' 'ere, after weshin' an' scrubbin' orl day, then mekkin' sum nice 'ash an' watter whelps for thee t' gobble darn, then ironin' that very shirt an' collar round y' neck. Ar

jus' felt like a nice quiet glass o' beer in't house, an' wot do a find, nearly on mi own dooarstep? Yor two canoodlin'!' Hidden from her view by the high side of the land settle, she towered above me and pointed a fat and not very clean accusing finger at Nellie and cried, 'As for you, madam, ar allus thowt you wor ennybody's for a gill o' beer!' Now that she was in full cry, nothing could stem the tirade, except shortage of breath, as she panted, 'Ar know nar why coil man teks s' long t' settle up when your owd feller's at work, an' that little bloody ginger-'eaded milkman's 'orse an' cart int artside orl that time fer nowt, ar'll bi bound. Painted 'ussy — y' nowt else!'

With that, she marched up to the table, Oliver cringing as she approached. Nellie's eyes opened wide with horror, fearing the worst. I held my breath — was I to be a witness to bloodshed? Mrs Gumson seized Nellie's drink, paused as if to throw it in the paramour's face, but instead she drank off the Guinness in one gulp. She turned her attention then to her husband. Grasping his full pint, she again took her time, holding the pot up high. Then with a magnificent gesture, she poured half the beer into her jug, knocked off Oliver's bowler and baptised him with the other half. He, once a figure of grace and charm on the ballroom floor, alehouse Lethario and breaker of hearts, sat there stunned as the beer ran over his brilliantined hair, down his nose and dripped off his sodden moustache.

Mechanically, he sucked at the drops, seemingly incapable of making any other movement. His wife, as if this act had exhausted her passion, sat down heavily at his side and took a swig out of the pitcher. The soothing effect of this potion appeared to please her, so she drank the rest, put down the jug on the table and regarded the chastened pair with the righteous superiority of an innocent, mistreated woman.

The trio sat there, oblivious of my presence in the darkening room as the fire burnt low, until Mrs Gumson spoke, addressing Nellie more patronisingly than with anger. 'Y' silly cow, y' ot ter 'av mooar sense at your age. Ar know my Oliver's gorra way wi' wimmin, 'e can't 'elp

it enny moor than a nice bit o' boiled 'am can stop attractin' bluebottles.' Nellie looked a trifle hurt at this comparison, but nodded in agreement, whilst Oliver, thankful that the wrath had subsided, wheedled, 'Ar know that luv, burra finished up wi' pick o' bunch, din't ar?' as he wiped away the beery tears from his face. 'Thi's nowt in it, 'onest, ar jus' 'appened ter bump inter Mrs Slatters an' asked 'er if she'd like a drink afoor ar went ter Buffs. That's reight, in't it?' the heart-throb appealed to Nellie, who spoke to Mrs Gumson as if he wasn't inbetween them. 'Y' know what your mester's like, he could charm a fairy off a Christmas tree, an' ar wor a bit upset, wot wi' that brick droppin' on ar owd feller's foot, a thowt a drink might cheer mi up a bit, like.'

Mrs Gumson, further mollified by the sight of her repentant spouse, digging in his trouser pocket and producing some money, mused, 'Ar know ony too well. Ar wor guin' art wi' a nice young bloke from Co-op when 'e', indicating Oliver with a sideways-turned thumb, 'cums arta blue an' sweeps mi off mi feet. Mi mother went barmy, burra couldn't do owt abart it, 'e wor jus' like Rufus Vaselino carryin' me off inter desert!' The sheikh went out to the bar and came back with a pint of bitter for himself, half a shandy for Nellie, and, as if to emphasise his wife's rightful place in his affections, a bottle of Bass, which he himself carefully decanted before presenting it to her.

As the lurid fires of lust and anger were quenched by ale, peace prevailed and the three sat closer together. Mrs Gumson was still a little stiff with moral righteousness; Oliver, the thwarted lover, had dried out and regained his colour and composure, whilst Nellie, frustrated though she must have been, kept stealing covert glances at Mrs Gumson until finally, unable to control her feelings any longer, blurted out to her friend, 'Tell y' wot, luv, when wi get back 'ooam, ar'll gie y' that tin o' salmon ar wor savin' fer mi weddin' anniversary!' This act of contrition affected Mrs Gumson to such an extent that she reached across Oliver's manly bread basket and patted Nellie's hand in a magnanimous gesture of forgiveness.

It was time for me to return to base, so taking advantage of the reconciliation, I slipped quietly and unobserved out of the pub and went back to my duties. A couple of frames of snooker, a chat and a little supper whiled away the time pleasantly enough, and about half past ten I decided to pay a call and retire to my bunk. The WCs were along an unlit corridor, but I knew the layout well enough. I was just buttoning up when I heard a racket in the street outside. By standing on the lavatory pan I could peer through the small, half-open window. The rain had ceased. It was now a moonlit night and below me I could plainly see Mr Gumson with Nellie hanging on to his arm, and clinging possessively to the other, swaying along the pavement, was his loving wife, carrying a jug of beer. Oliver's untutored bass contrasted nicely against Mrs Gumson's tuneless contralto and Nellie's strident falsetto in a spirited rendering of 'When They Sound the Last All Clear'!

If the singing wasn't in harmony, at least *they* appeared to be, as I watched their unsteady progress down Clarence Street, until the last notes faded away and I returned to my post.

Chapter 26

Posted

Nineteen forty-four. I was twenty, the war had been raging for five years and, soon after my birthday, I came home from work to find a long buff envelope with the letters 'O.H.M.S.' embossed on it, addressed to me. Mam's face was drawn with worry. My brother had been wounded in the fierce fighting in Italy and, although he had recovered and was back in the line, like many people at home the sight of that envelope nearly always meant bad news, although not so much as the dreaded telegram.

I ripped it open with trembling fingers. Had I been called to the colours at last? Even though the Allies and the Russians were gaining ground and thousands of planes were bombing the Third Reich, of which Göring had once boasted that 'not a single enemy bomb would fall on the Fatherland', the Japanese were still strongly entrenched in the Far East and it looked as though the fighting would continue there for years.

The thin sheet of paper took some getting out of the envelope without tearing. As I read the closely-typewritten orders, I didn't know whether to feel relieved or disappointed. It stated in a few terse sentences that George Cunningham was to report at 7.00 hours, September 28, 101 Battery rocket projector site at Shirecliffe. When I broke the news to Mam she was less upset, but still worried. 'Shirecliffe?' she said, 'That's a long way. Are you sure you'll be alright?' Considering that millions of men were being transported thousands of miles all over the world on land, air and sea, I felt that I could find my way to Shirecliffe, even though that side of the city was as unknown to me as

China. Attendances at all Home Guard units had, for some years, been compulsory: only a doctor's certificate or a bereavement could count as an excuse. Non-attenders were fined, and, in some extreme cases, sent to prison. A few days before I was to embark, the War Office announced that all manning of rocket projectors would become voluntary.

A sense of duty and perhaps the fear of being fined impelled me to put on my uniform and kit and set off for Shirecliffe. Although I had slept away from home many nights on fire watching duties, this was somehow different.

I had mixed feelings of apprehension as I entered the gates of the gun site and reported at the guard house and was directed to 'A' Battery. I marched along the bleak hillside until I came to the first line of rocket projectors. Eight of them formed 'A' battery, and very menacing they looked, especially to me, who had only seen the solitary practice one at the Somme Barracks.

I walked down the line and then found my way to a Nissen hut which bore the emblem 'No. 1 "A" BATTERY' on the door. There was no reply to my knocking, so I entered, trying to appear as if I was an old hand at Army life. The hut was empty. Ten bunks were ranged down one side and an equal number opposite, with a big iron Tortoise stove in the middle of the floor. A couple of tables and a few stools comprised the furnishings, and photos of film stars cut from magazines plastered on the walls provided an interesting decor. One of them in particular caught my attention. It was Veronica Lake, a vamp with a mane of blonde hair called a 'peek-boo-bang', because it covered half her face and gave her a 'see if you dare' expression, much copied by thousands of girls. It was very popular, but many accidents were caused by the hairstyle. In fact at Viner's, Mary Hancock, who looked smashing with it, lost most of her hair and some of her scalp around the chuck of a drilling machine. After that the Government made it compulsory for women to wear over their crowning glory something called a snood: a posh name for a hairnet.

I sat on the edge of a bunk and laid down my gas mask and steel helmet. The time passed slowly. After about an hour of checking my watch and listening in vain for a footstep passing the door, suddenly a bell rang, startlingly loud, amplified by the steel walls of the Nissen. I jumped to my feet. The bell went on ringing as I ran round the hut trying to trace the source. In a blinding flash of the obvious, I made for a telephone on the far wall. Lifting the receiver, I muttered 'Hello?' A voice that nearly shattered my eardrums shouted, '"A" Battery, get me Lieutenant Shaw.' 'Sorry,' I replied, regaining my military composure, 'I'm afraid he's not here.' Immediately came another request: 'Put Sergeant Smelter on then.' Again I had to apologise for his absence, to be met by a demand for Bombardier Bowker. Once more I replied in the negative. The voice at the other end of the line enquired exasperatedly, ''Oo *is* theer then?' I answered meekly, 'Me.' ''Oo the bloody 'ell's me?' shouted the irate voice. 'Gunner Cunningham,' I answered. A short silence followed before the dialogue continued. 'Ar many mooar on yer?' When I replied tersely in my best military matter, 'Nobdy,' the phone at the other end was plonked down and I was left staring blankly at the hushed receiver.

There seemed nothing to do but retire to my bunk and sit on it. However, I hadn't long to ponder whose voice had been speaking at the other end of the line. A rapid clatter of boots on the concrete path outside the hut culminated when the door was thrown open and the burly figure of a sergeant major framed the aperture. He gazed at me then glared around the otherwise unoccupied hut. 'Weer is everybody?' he demanded. I jumped to attention. 'I don't know, I've been here an hour and nobody's come in.' Suddenly, the SM's expression softened into the semblance of a smile. 'Ar know wot it is. A couple o' days ago it were announced that it wor voluntary to attend, an' this is wot's 'appened. There's ony thee turned up arta 'ole battery.' He pushed his forage cap to the back of his head and had a good scratch at his bristly noddle, possibly in an attempt to get his brain working, until he finally made a decision which, although it wouldn't have much effect on the worldwide conflict, pleased both him and me. 'Get thissen o'er ter NAAFI. It's darn far end o' site near sum big trees. Tha'll not need thi gas mask, but tek thi tin 'at in case it's rainin' when tha cums back. Tha can stop 'til chuckin art time. If thi's owt guin' off, ar'll know weer t' find thi.'

The inside of the big wooden NAAFI hut was bright and cheerful behind the blackout curtains and a pint of beer raised my spirits somewhat. I sat down in a corner and looked around. Apart from the girls behind the bar, the only others were three sergeants and a small grey-haired old chap sitting on his own at a table near to mine. Feeling sorry for him, I went over and asked him if he'd have a drink, as his pot was nearly empty. His face lit up and I fetched a couple of pints and joined him. He looked too old and frail to be in the Home Guard and seemed to have little to say for himself, so I regaled him with my heroic exploits, the blitz, fire watching, the bomb throwing in the park, and the rigours of training nights at the Somme Barracks. At the mention of this name he looked a little pensive, but cheered up when I bought him another pint. I was enjoying myself, telling him more and more of my exploits in the war. He asked me, but didn't press the matter, to have a drink, but I insisted on paying for two more. He seemed to be very interested in what I was saying, never interrupting, but just adding an 'Oo, ar' now and again. At ten o'clock, time was called and I shook hands with the old fellow, patting him on the back with the familiarity of a comrade in arms who had seen some service.

I marched back to my battery. There they were, gleaming in the moonlight, eight of them capable of firing sixteen high-explosive shells, and I alone was in sole charge of them.

I walked round and round my battery with hands clasped behind my back in typical officer style, savouring every moment of my single-handed defence of Sheffield, until Nature called and I retreated to the latrines. Before I turned in, I made a final inspection, half wishing that the sirens would sound. I chuckled when an episode came into my mind from one of Charlie Chaplin's films, called *Shoulder Arms*. He was the sole survivor after a battle, so he tied four rifles with fixed bayonets on to a plank and marched up the trench with them showing above the parapet, ducked down at the end, ran back then marched up again with the rifles showing, deluding Jerry into thinking that massive reinforcements were arriving. I would look alright, loading, elevating, aiming and firing one rocket projector, let alone a battery of eight.

Regretfully, I retired to my solitary quarters, laid fully clothed on a bunk and drifted into sleep. A squadron of Nazi dive bombers attacked the gun site, destroying every gun except mine. Sticks of bombs exploded all around me, but I remained steadfast at my position and with a final gesture of defiance, shooting down the leading Stuka with my last remaining rocket. I was in the midst of being buried with full military honours, when a stentorian voice rudely resurrected me by bawling, '"A" Battery, action stations!' Rolling out of the bunk, startled out of my wits and wondering where I was, I beheld the gallant sergeant major laughing his head off in the doorway. He was in good humour in spite of the early hour.

The reason became evident when he said, 'Cum on, let's go an 'av sum breakfast, it's mar last neet up 'eer, an' it's thine, so wi might as well celebrate.' We strolled across the site more like workmates than a gunner and his sergeant, when an officer, fully uniformed and obviously making for home, approached us. 'Mornin' Hobson,' he said in a friendly manner, as he returned our salutes. 'Looks like the last night for the old battery, eh? Who's this young chap?' Hobson replied, 'Cunningham, sir, 'e's only one 'oo turned up in number one battery.' The officer, freshly shaved and smart, smiled and remarked, 'Good show, lad.' Turning to the sergeant he said, 'Get yourselves down to

Geo. Cunningham

the NAAFI and have a breakfast on me. Tell Gladys to put it on my bill. Cunningham has earned it. I'm sure he would have given a good account of himself if anything had happened during the night. Morning.' He touched his cap peak with a short swagger cane and marched away.

Puffed with pride, I entered the NAAFI hut. It was deserted, except for the little old chap from the night before, sitting at a table in the corner as if he had been there since then. He acknowledged my greeting with a friendly nod as the sergeant and I took our breakfasts over to a table near the stove. The toast and dripping and scalding hot tea tasted good and I wolfed down four slices, not a word passing between us until the last crumb was finished. Hobson leaned back in his chair and lit a Park Drive, inhaled and blew a plume of smoke up to the ceiling. I got two more mugs of tea and also bought one for the old chap, who accepted it with a friendly smile and a polite 'Ta'.

I felt a bit sorry for him and hoped I hadn't overawed him with last night's stories, and perhaps he had also heard of my solo command of number one battery. 'Who is that old bloke?' I enquired of the sergeant. He looked at me in disbelief. 'Dun't tha know 'im? 'E's got mooar flippin' medals dan Fry's flippin' cocoa! 'E joined up in 1914 an' wor in all big battles — Marne, and Wipers. Thi reckon 'e wor first man ter top o' Hill 60, then 'e wor wi City Battalion on Somme in that big push in 1916. 'E stopped one at Passchendaele, burree wor back in line after a few days an' den finished up alongside Canadians, tekkin Cambrai in 1918.' Hobson lit another fag and carried on. 'Owd Charlie never sez owt, burrit wor orl abart 'im in Telegraph after waar. 'E got M.M. an' D.C.M. an' thi reckon 'e should a' got V.C. Even Froggies gen 'im a couple o' gongs.' I looked across the room at the warrior, who raised his mug in a friendly manner. I replied likewise, a trifle deflated to say the least.

Chapter 27

The End of a Romance

*I*N EARLY December 1944, the War Office, no doubt satisfied that I had done all that could reasonably be expected of me, stated that the Home Guard was to be stood down. On a wet Sunday morning, I and my comrades in arms packed the Regent Picture House in Barker's Pool to hear the King's message of appreciation read out. Afterwards, we paraded around the rain-soaked streets, past the gaunt skeleton girders and bleak bomb sites. In spite of the weather and being wet through, our steps were firm and joyful in anticipation of the peaceful years to come. Christmas arrived. Strangely enough, although it seemed that victory was in sight, I felt vaguely miserable, now that the fire watching and Home Guard duties were finished. As usual in times like that, I sought solace with my friend John Barleycorn.

I walked up The Moor one Saturday evening. It was strange to see lights, albeit dim, and no blackout curtains on the door of the Traveller's Rest. In spite of years of war and surviving the blitz which had destroyed most of the nearby shops, the place was clean and bright and the bar looked well stocked, even if most of the bottles were dummies. Billy Lee the landlord, immaculate as ever with a flower in his buttonhole, greeted his customers as they entered. Palm trees in pots and Christmas decorations, bunches of holly and mistletoe lifted my spirits, as did the pint of Gilmour's bitter. I stood in the passage, wondering what the future would bring, when through the door came the stocky khaki-clad figure of a sergeant, accompanied by a young woman. Before I could take much notice of her, she, with her back to me, hurried into the ladies', her high heels clicking on the mosaic floor. I gazed casually at the soldier and my blood ran cold. It was none other than Jimmy Wrathfull, my erstwhile schoolmate, tormentor and eventually vanquished foe. As he ordered drinks, a pint of beer and a milk stout, I gazed at his barrel chest and the beefy hands on the bar and wondered if I could make an undetected exit. No such luck; he turned and looked me full in the face. Recognition was instant. His instinctive glare of aggression was replaced by a grin as he grasped me by the hand and crushed my fingers with a bone-crunching gesture of goodwill. 'Ar do, Georgie,' he growled, 'Merry Christmas.' Stifling a yelp of pain and blinking away tears of agony, I squeaked, 'All the best, Jim.'

He looked fit and well and told me he was home on leave from France. For something to say, now that the pain in my fingers had diminished somewhat, I asked him if he had heard anything about Harry Flathers and Albert Moxay. He laughed and replied, 'Flathers got sent ter Borstal for three years for pinchin' coil, an' when he cum art, Government made 'im a Bevin boy an' sent 'im darn pit. Thi'll be plenty o' stuff darn theer for 'im ter nick.' We both turned as a click of heels heralded the return of Jack's girlfriend.

The second shock of the evening was greater than the first. A crown of Titian hair, bewitching eyes and a titillating smile stunned me. It was Molly Moxay. Her ruby lips parted to reveal twin rows of sparkling white teeth as she spoke in dulcet tones that sent an amorous quiver down my spine. ''Ow are y'?' she fluted. 'Long time no see.' I mumbled

something about being busy, what with war work and so on, trying to recover and come to terms with the fact that the girl of my dreams was consorting with the enemy. To give myself more time, I blurted out, 'How's your Albert?' She laughed, displaying to their full advantage her pearly eating tackle. 'Oh, 'im!' she giggled. 'Last time we 'eeard, 'e wor in Italy, doin' a bit o' field punishment fer knockin' off tins o' grub from Yanks.' In spite of her joviality, I sensed that underneath the levity there lurked a spark of sentiment and that she wasn't really happy to be with Jim.

She brought out a paper packet of Woodbines from her handbag and gave one to Jimmy, without offering them to me. So, she remembers that I don't smoke — at least she hadn't forgotten that. A tremble of her fingers, the constant nervous flicking of cigarette ash betrayed her agitation and I surprised her when I caught her looking sideways at me with an appealing glance, as if regretting that we couldn't be together.

As usual, in situations such as these, I was lost for words, only thinking afterwards what I should have said and done. Molly had never looked lovelier, not even on that moonlit night when passions had flamed high, especially when our eyes met again and she smiled, though she accompanied it by a meaningful shrug of her shoulders, as if to imply that we were in the grip of an irresistible force beyond our control.

Sergeant Wrathfull too must have been affected, because he rasped, 'Cum on Moll, let's gu sumweer a bit mooar livelier, it's like a bloody morgue in 'eer!' The swine stubbed out his fag and encircled that tender, willowy waist possessively with his beastly, muscular arm. Molly looked up at me. Were those tears that were misting the blue of those adorable eyes? Perhaps an unspoken plea to be rescued from the grasp of the ogre? Or could it just be cigarette smoke? At that poignant, fateful moment of destiny, I made a tentative gesture to take her by the arm, but Jack steered her firmly down the passage. She turned and reached out a hand, imploringly. I stood dithering at the bar, unable to move, then the light of my life was yanked unceremoniously through the door — gone forever.

131

Chapter 28

Victory in Europe (and Clarence Lane)

THE FIRST few weeks of 1945 were bitterly cold, with thirty degrees of frost. Fuel was short, but an unexpected bonus was open lorries, full of a black sludge-like cargo of slurry, which was the residue from coal-washing plants. One of the lorries pulled up outside Viner's and I dashed out and filled two buckets full for a tanner. Back in the die shop, I moulded the mess into balls as big as an orange. These I placed on a wire grill over the gas ring and left them to dry. They burnt feebly but at least with a little warmth when I took them home. Nearly every house in the district used them and for days a pall of dark smoke hung over the streets. In spite of hardship, there was a general feeling of relief as if everyone sensed that the long ordeal would soon be over.

Spring came at last and Mussolini and his mistress departed, ending their lives hanging upside down on a gas lamp. Adolf made his exit from the world two days later, and his wife took poison, thus reversing the old joke about the woman who said to a man who had offended her in some way, 'If you were my husband, I'd give you poison,' to which the miscreant replied, 'Madam, if I were married to you, I'd take it!'

So, after nearly six years of conflict, peace returned to Europe. Bunting hung across every street. Banners made from old sheets bearing slogans like the one for my brother which I painted, saying 'Welcome home, Billy', were displayed on many houses — the luckier ones, that is. Although the pain of parting from Molly lingered, a general feeling of exciting anticipation in the air was infectious.

One evening I strolled aimlessly along Moore Street and decided to have a quick one in the Earl Grey. It was only just turned eight o'clock on the big timepiece over the door, but already quite a few customers were standing at the bar. I got a pint of Tennant's bitter and took a seat in the little bay window snug looking out on to Ecclesall Road. A man, the only occupant, gazed at me rather vacantly until mutual recognition dawned. It was Mr Millichip, my father's one-time traveller, salesman and friend of my boyhood.

He was smartly clad in a brown suit, stiff white collar and a knitted tie, but he himself was rather the worse for wear. His eyes were glassy and his speech slurred as he greeted me with tipsy familiarity. 'Ar do, Georgie, housh it goin'?' I sat on a stool opposite to him and enquired what he had been doing, as I hadn't seen him for years. 'Awl reight,' he proudly replied, 'Ar went back inter big worksh an' arve bin gerrin some good money.' I noticed that his cap, a snappy eight-panel job, was resting on his head at an unusual angle, the neb being in the region of his right ear. Before I could comment on this, he took a long swig of beer which emptied his pint pot, then he took off his cap, threw it up in the air, caught it and replaced it on his head and gave it a clockwise turn, rather like tightening a nut, so that the peak pointed backwards. On completing this manoeuvre, he remarked with great satisfaction, 'Happy landingsh!' The landlord, Billy Downes, watched this performance with amusement and approbation, as he pulled another pint for Jack. I went to the bar to fetch it and asked Billy what was going on.

'Oh,' he chuckled, 'Owd Jack carries on like this every birthday. When he downs a pint, 'e gies 'is cap a turn. It gus round 'is 'eead six times befooar it's back weear 'e started. This is second time round. It dun't do any 'arm, but it does me a bit o' good.'

I left Mr Millichip still performing his mysterious ritual and wandered into the street, debating whether to have a drink at Tommy Green's. I was just about to lift the sneck on the dram shop door, when I noticed some activity down the 'Owd Lane'. It was a 'Victory in Europe' party. Although the Japs were still holding out in the Far East, the fact that the arch-enemy Adolf had bit the dust at last made everybody feel like celebrating. Tables and chairs had been brought into the lane. Planks on boxes, and even lavatory doors taken off their hinges and covered with paper, made makeshift supports for the food and drink, which miraculously appeared from long-cherished hoards. Streamers hung across our old football pitch and along the walls bordering the back yards, while the 'Owd foundry' was decorated up like a fairy palace.

All the seats had been taken up by kids and a few older people, but I was happy to stand at the back. Tommy Green, landlord of the Oxford House, had sent down some bottles of beer and a glass of it was pressed into my hand by Mrs Gumson, who insisted on giving me a kiss.

She appeared to have been celebrating for some time, because suddenly she seized hold of Nellie Slatters and the pair of them performed a spirited can-can on the causey outside the foundry gates. What they lacked in style and grace was compensated for by the energy they put into the provocative dance. Nellie, overpowered by the size and weight of her partner, was content to hang on, merely lifting her legs high enough to display a patched petticoat and lisle stockings, darned at the knees. Not so the magnificent Mrs Gumson. Probably with memories of hectic nights long ago — and inspired by Mr Gumson who whistled piercingly with two fingers in his mouth, only removed to shout words of encouragement such as 'Gu on mi owd luv, gie 'em a treat'

133

— she lifted her skirts and kicked her fat legs in the air, revealing a pair of bloomers which billowed like barrage balloons. The finale, which came all too soon after a series of tremendous high kicks, ended the performance when she spun around, flounced her clothes shoulder high and bent herself almost double, thus exposing an enormous backside, covered tightly in silvery material which had a crown and the letters 'W.D.' stamped upon it.

During the clapping and cheering that followed, Mrs Gumson collapsed onto a chair, and panted to her husband, 'Get mi a drink, arm fair gaggin!' I heard behind me a woman's shrill voice, tinged with derision, but also envy, remark to a companion, 'Did ta see wot 'er britches wor made on? Bleedin' parachute silk, that's wot it wer. Ar wonder ar many jumps she 'ad ter gerrall that!'

Conviviality reigned supreme. Many long-standing neighbourly feuds and back yard quarrels were forgotten in the long-awaited day of peace.

Not all of them, it seemed. I turned at a touch on my elbow. It was Norman Blackwell, accompanied by his father, the intrepid stormer of Pickering's on that first night of war. 'Nar den, Georgie, it's a good do, in't it?' remarked Norman, as someone passed him a bun. His father, though, didn't appear to be all that impressed by the celebrations. 'Ar wonder wot 'appened t' fire watching money,' he said morosely to no one in particular. I knew this sum of cash had been a bone of contention in the district for some months. Ever since the blitz, almost five years ago, a weekly collection had taken place in each street to purchase fire fighting equipment, mainly ladders, which weren't provided by the authorities. Our particular fund had been organised by Billy Podson's father, whose family had moved up the social scale from Green Street to the dizzy heights of Clarence Street. He was very punctual, never missing a Friday, meticulously jotting down in a little notebook the coppers donated by every household.

Mr Blackwell's observation hadn't gone unheeded. 'Thart reight, Albert,' said Alf Thompson, the man next to him. 'Thi must 'av bin a good few quid in t' fund an' nobdy's ever seen a ladder, as thar, Ernest?' he appealed to his companion, who shook his head emphatically. The topic was taken up by the older people standing at the back of the tables, each one claiming that they had contributed more than the other. Suddenly, someone on the fringe of our crowd of dissenters cried softly, 'Ey up, look wot's cummin!' All eyes turned to a little group of people walking up the lane. It was headed by Mr Podson, a bow-legged man, whose east and west visionary affliction made it obvious that Billy was indeed the fruit of his loins. Linking his arm possessively was his lady wife, a roly-poly little woman, the brightness of her lipstick admirably matched by lurid patches of rouge on her cheeks. It wasn't the make-up or the flower-bedecked hat perched at a coquettish angle on her newly-permed hair that drew the attention of some of the women, however. One of them, Mrs Garfitt, folding her arms tightly across her meagre bosom as if to compress her agitation, pursed her lips and with brow wrinkled in concentration, she peered pointedly at the approaching party. 'Look at that fur cooat she's gorron,' she exclaimed to Mrs Gumson, who had taken a beverage and was modestly arranging her dress. 'Thi's a bob or two's worth theer. Ar bet that's weer ar bloody ladder money's gone. It's on 'er back!'

Mrs Podson, unaware of the hostility that this remark had brought about, beamed patronisingly at everyone, confident in her sartorial superiority. ''Ello,' she said in a friendly manner, 'Enjoyin' yersens are y'?' Mrs Gumson, never a believer in preliminary trivialities or polite gambits, came straight to the point and answered, 'Not as much as we would be, if we 'ad *our* ladder money ter spend, instead on it keepin' *you* warm, madam!' It was evident to everyone that the arrow had struck home. A guilty blush suffused the already-rosy cheeks of Mrs Podson, as she struggled to find words to defend herself against this accusation. Her husband, too, was visibly affected, although he had an advantage of not having to look anyone straight in the eye. 'Nay, nay,' he mumbled, 'Ar bowt it art o' mi o'ertime money, din't ar luv?' His wife, at a loss for words, merely nodded. Mrs Gumson, not to be fobbed off, cried, 'Right, y' only live round corner, nip along an' bring us ar cash, den!' Mr Podson, taken aback by this demand, falteringly stuttered, 'Ar carn't, it's in a special account in Yorkshire Penny Bank.' His spouse, thinking the pressure was off, smiled superciliously. It was evident that they had both gravely underestimated Mrs Gumson. 'Gu an' fetch us bank book, then,' she cried triumphantly, 'An we'll soon see 'oo's reight!'

The chorus of approval from non-playing bystanders convinced Mrs Podson that the game was up, so she abandoned rhetoric and gave Mrs Gumson a violent shove in that lady's ample bosom. At the same time she shrieked, 'Cum arta rooad, ar've got mooar t' do than argue toss wi you in street, y' owd cow!'

Once again she miscalculated the power of her opponent, who cried, 'O, o, missis, that's ar y' want ter play is it?' promptly seizing Mrs Podson's hair and shaking it so violently that the lady's hat fell off. Her husband attempted to intervene, but was deterred by Mr Gumson, who squared up to him in the approved prizefighter style and issued an invitation to 'Cum on den, let's 'av thi.' Billy Podson, who with a girlfriend had brought up the rear of the party, pushed forward to give his parents filial support, but was prevented by Norman, who made a fist, blew on it and gave it a rub, before pointedly holding it aloft. Billy turned his head sideways, trying to focus on me as he had done on that long-ago voting day. I relived the terror as if it had been yesterday, but thankfully he backed off and Mr Blackwell, with the assistance of two men, parted the contestants, who were running out of steam anyway. Mrs Podson, who a few minutes earlier had been the epitome of fashion, was tousled and tear-stained as she tried to knock back some shape into her hat which had been trampled underfoot in the melee.

Stifling a sob and wiping her nose with an upward gesture of an open palm, she confessed, 'Ar'm sorry, ar've bin wantin' a fur cooat all mi life, an' when this bloke said 'e could get one on black market, ma mester said 'e'd gerrit fo' me arta ladder money. 'E'll pay yer all back, waint y' luv?' Mr Podson, relieved that he hadn't had to indulge in fisticuffs, replied, 'As God's mi judge, ar will,' and looked for someone to shake hands with, finally settling on Mr Blackwell, who, although he returned the gesture, remarked menacingly, 'Tha better.'

The Podsons were allowed through the throng, having to run the gauntlet of remarks such as 'Tha wants ter tek that cooat o' thine up t' Marsdens on Button Lane. Thi gie y' a penny apiece fer owd rabbit skins!' Mrs Gumson, the worthy champion of a righteous cause, sat back in a chair, every inch the magnanimous victor, and was regaled with a glass of Magnet, which she drank off with relish, declaring, 'Ar've bin wantin' ter gie that brassy bitch a good shekkin ever sin' that dog o' hers mucked on mar dooarstep, an' very same neet in Tommy Green's ar copped 'er mekkin' sheep's eyes at my Oliver.'

All of a sudden I saw, standing alone on the fringe of the crowd, Edgar Colcutt, the friend and mentor of my childhood. He was dressed for the occasion in a green-with-age frock coat, baggy flannels and a straw boater with a tram ticket stuck in the band, and stood staring vacantly but good-humourdly at the happy gathering. I felt a pang of guilt at not making any attempt to visit him during the war, so I went over and enquired how he had been keeping. 'A bower quiet for me and a sleep full of sweet dreams, health and quiet breathing,' he replied, adding dryly, 'Keats, Endymion, in case you have forgotten.' All I could do was apologise for my absence and make a promise to renew our friendship now that hostilities had ceased. He thanked me courteously, then remarked, a trifle sarcastically, I thought, 'Peace hath her victories, no less renowned than those of war.'

A little chastened, I helped carry back home some of the tables and chairs, now that the party was breaking up. Mr Blackwell, Oliver and Mrs Gumson, and the faithful Nellie, whom I had heard earlier apologising for the absence of her husband, stating that ''E wor working fer

Government at Wakefield, an' wunt bi 'ooam fer three months', declared their intention of 'avin' a jar in the Lincoln, Mr Broadley's pub in Clarence Street. I walked in the twilight down the Owd Lane with Norman, turned the corner at Polly Brady's shop and through force of habit made for the corner shop. Just as we reached the step, a blaze of neon lights illuminated all the front of the Co-op, the first time for six years. 'That's a good sign,' exclaimed Norman, ever the optimist, 'Ar bet it'll bi a fine day tomorra!'

Another harbinger of good times ahead was the sound of a raucous rendering of 'Lily Marlene', delivered flatly but with gusto and apparently performed by a duo. Both voices were strangely familiar, even though distorted by drink, and, coincidentally with the words of the song, two figures passed under the light of a lantern, not by the barrack gate, but a gas lamp in Clarence Street.

I recognised, as they clung together with arms around each other's shoulders, reaching for even higher notes, Albert Moxay and Harry Flathers. They both let out a homecoming whoop of greeting as they drew near. Albert was in khaki, and browned by a sun hotter than we ever knew in this country, but Flathers was blanched white as a stick of celery, no doubt due to his underground activities. Both were in excellent spirits, and smelling of them too, as they shook hands with Norman

and me. 'I on'y landed dis mornin',' cried Moxay, 'Ar've bin orl o'er shant, North Africa, Sicily, Italy. Wot yor been up to?'

Flathers, not to be outdone but still with his old habit of looking backwards to see if he could be overheard, confided hoarsely, 'Di sent me up ter a pit in Durham. Fooaks wor reight enuff, danose, burra cudden't mek art wot di wor clackin' abart. Tha'd a' thowt thi'd tork same as me an' dee wunt da?'

Moxay took out a pack of Camels, gave one to Flathers, then suddenly he shouted, 'Arberra can still gerra leet fer nowt!' and promptly shinned like a monkey up the gas lamp, straddled the crossbar, pushed the fag up to the mantle, lit it, then slid down to land lightly on his feet. He took a deep drag, exhaled and again enquired how I had gone on during the war. My Home Guard and fire watching exploits would have sounded trivial compared to the adventures that he, and even Flathers, must have had. Norman, too, had little to brag about, having spent the war years bent over a lathe in an engineering works on Harrow Street, so speaking for both of us, I replied, 'There hasn't been much doing at all round here' and left it at that. The pair of them were determined to make a night of it, agreeing that their next port of call would be Harry Gilchrist's pub at the corner of Milton Street. In spite of their plea to 'Cum on, let's mek a neet on it', we declined the invitation and the duo stumbled up Clarence Street, singing a novel arrangement of 'We'll Meet Again', pausing every now and again to argue about the proper words.

As the din died away, quietness settled down once more on the street corner. Lights appeared in house windows; Mrs Freeman let her cat out; Edgar appeared at his door to have a last gaze at the solar system before locking up, leaving Norman and me, two of us where once there had been three, standing as we had done so many times on the old corner shop doorstep.

A plane droned high overhead, a presence no longer a cause for fear. We both stared upwards until its friendly lights winked away into the heavenly vault, and the silence that followed seemed even more profound.

'I wish owd Vinny could have made it,' murmured Norman, echoing my thoughts. He took his leave and I was left alone on the old stone step, reflecting that at the age of twenty, after six years of tumultuous events and tremendous battles, I had come out of it as a half-trained die-sinker, a fire watcher who had never doused a conflagration, a part-time soldier who hadn't fired a shot, a bookie's runner who couldn't back a winner, and a thwarted lover.

Vincent Crookes (Vinny)
1924–1943